THE WORKS OF ALEXANDER RADCLIFFE (1696)

A FACSIMILE REPRODUCTION
WITH AN INTRODUCTION BY
KEN ROBINSON

SCHOLARS' FACSIMILES & REPRINTS
DELMAR, NEW YORK 12054
1981

SCHOLARS' FACSIMILES & REPRINTS
ISSN 0161-7729
SERIES ESTABLISHED 1936
VOLUME 365

Published by
Scholars' Facsimiles & Reprints
Delmar, New York 12054

Printed in the U.S.A.

Library of Congress Cataloging in Publication Data

Radcliffe, Alexander, fl. 1669-1696.
The works of Alexander Radcliffe (1696)

Reprint: Originally published: The works of Alex.
Radcliffe. 3rd ed., augm. London: Printed for R. Wellington, 1696.
Includes bibliographical references.
I. Robinson, Ken. II. Title.
PR3056.R15 1981 821'.4 81-9003
ISBN 0-8201-1365-4 AACR2

INTRODUCTION

From the *DNB* to the Yale edition of *Poems on Affairs of State* Alexander Radcliffe has been thought of as a "disciple of the Earl of Rochester in verse." There are good grounds for believing that his contemporaries, too, thought of him in much the same way. At least, whoever was responsible for the "1680" edition of Rochester tried to pass off poems by Radcliffe as Rochester's. The received reason for linking the two poets is trivial, that Radcliffe "rivalled his master in ribaldry";[1] but there are more important points of comparison and contrast in both the life and works.

Like Rochester, Radcliffe stemmed from a strong Royalist line. His grandfather had been honoured as K.B. at the remarkably early age of seventeen, when he carried the purple robe at the coronation of Charles I.[2] He was to repay his king's favour with loyal service in the Civil War, fighting at Edgehill, where he was wounded and taken prisoner. After a spell in the Tower he was released on bail in August 1643, moved to his house in Chancery Lane,[3] and eventually returned to his estate at Ordsall in Lancashire in 1654, where he died in the same year. His military example was followed by two of his sons, Alexander, his namesake, and Sussex. Both enlisted as boys. Sussex died at High Holbourn in 1649 as a result of wounds suffered the year before at the battle of Ribble Bridge; Alexander, the poet's

1. See *DNB* and *Poems on Affairs of State. Augustan Satirical Verse, 1660-1714. Vol. 2: 1678-1681*, ed. Elias F. Mengel, Jr. (New Haven, 1965), p. 110.

2. For this account of Radcliffe and the Radcliffes, see *DNB;* Charles P. Hampson, *The Book of the Radclyffes* (Edinburgh, 1940), esp. pp. 166-71; *Burke's Landed Gentry*, 18th ed., 3 vols. (London, 1972), III, 742; and *Poems on Affairs of State. . . .Vol. 6: 1697-1704*, ed. Frank H. Ellis (New Haven, 1970), p. 165. Errors in these accounts are corrected silently.

3. *CJ*, III, 217. For the location of Sir Alexander's house, see *Calendar of the Committee for Advanced Money*, I, 527.

father, was more fortunate. Despite his youth (b. 1633) he acquitted himself with such gallantry that he was quickly promoted to the rank of captain. Like Rochester's father, he was with Charles at Worcester in 1651, and after the defeat he fled to Holland, remaining in exile until the Restoration, when he returned to an estate at Hampstead. The fortunes of the Ordsall Radcliffes had been depleted by recusancy fines, the expenses of war, and sequestration.[4] When John, the first son, succeeded his father in 1654, the estate was mortgaged to the hilt, so that by 1657 he had to sell up. There was little for Alexander to return to at the Restoration, and the Restoration settlement provided scant compensation. When Dame Jane Radcliffe, the poet's grandmother, petitioned Charles in 1665 for a pension "in consideration of the services and sufferings of . . . her late husband," it was recommended that since "there would be no end to such pensions" she should receive "a payment of royal bounty for her present reliefe"; but there is no record of any payment.[5] By contrast, Charles met Rochester's reminder of his claims to favour as "Wilmot's son" with a pension of £500 per annum and later, in 1666, with office at court as a Gentleman of the Bedchamber, which brought an additional annuity of £1,000.[6] Radcliffe, presumably born out of England, had to look to a profession to make his way in the world. He first turned to the law, entering Gray's Inn 12 November 1669, but he was not called to the Bar.[7] He had perhaps already begun to write, for a

4. On 6 May 1645 the Commons agreed to discharge and take off the sequestration of Sir Alexander's estate (*CJ*, IV, 133). This seems to have applied only to his Lancashire and Norfolk estates (see *Calendar of the Proceedings of the Committee for Compounding*, I, 95 and 116; and Hampson, p. 166). It is impossible to tell what influence the Radcliffes' Catholic background had on the poet, but three points should be noted: i) the oblique reflection on the Test Acts in the song "*To the Tune of* Per fas per nefas"; ii) Radcliffe dedicated *The Ramble* to Annesley in 1682; iii) Colonel Fitzgerald, under whom Radcliffe served from 1672, was a notorious Catholic.

5. *CTB: 1660-67*, p. 674.

6. *The Complete Poems of John Wilmot, Earl of Rochester*, ed. David M. Vieth (Hew Haven, 1968), p. 155 (as Vieth points out, the reminder may have been written by Robert Whitehall).

7. *The Register of Admissions to Gray's Inn 1521-1889*, ed. Joseph Foster (London, 1889), p. 307.

contemporary manuscript version of his "The Ramble" bears the date 1668,[8] and probably by 20 March 1672/3 he had established himself as "a Gray's Inn wit." Rochester perhaps refers to him in his "A Ramble in St. James's Park" as

> A great inhabiter of the pit,
> Where critic-like he sits and squints,
> Steals pocket handkerchiefs, and hints,
> From's neighbour, and the comedy,
> To court, and pay, his landlady.[9]

Beside this unflattering picture belongs the caricature in "A Satire on the Times" from which Radcliffe emerges as "Punkrid".[10] He was clearly feeling his way into fashionable libertine life as well as the literary world, and despite the apparently straitened finances of his family he seems to have been well provided for. Looking back in 1682 he could comment that "*many of these things* [the poems in *The Ramble*] *were wrote several years ago, when Youth and too much Money represented Extravagance a Virtue.*"

By the time that Rochester's poem was written, Radcliffe had probably turned from the law to a military career. In March 1672 he acquired a captaincy in Colonel John Fitzgerald's regiment of foot, a post for which he seems to have been suited by temperament as well as family tradition.[11] To Giles Jacob "he was a Man of strong propensity to Mirth and Pleasure, as generally most of our Military Gentlemen are."[12] Despite abandoning his legal studies Radcliffe remained a frequenter of Gray's Inn.[13] In 1681 (15 June) he was involved in an affray

8. See David M. Vieth, *Attribution in Restoration Poetry* (New Haven, 1963), p. 473.

9. *The Complete Poems*, p. 42. It is possible that Rochester is offering a general character.

10. *The Poetical Works of the Earls of Rochester, Roscommon and Dorset*, 2 vols. (London, 1757), I, 19.

11. Charles Dalton, *English Army Lists and Commission Registers, 1661-1741* (London, 1892-1904), I, 119.

12. *The Poetical Register*, 2 vols. (London, 1723), II, 170.

13. It may be that he continued to lodge in Gray's Inn (see William R. Douthwaite, *Gray's Inn Its History & Associations* [London, 1886], p. xvi). An A. Radcliffe is mentioned as living in St. Martin in the Fields in 1679 (*CTB: 1679-80*, p. 262), but this could be any one of several men of this name.

there when "severall gentlemen of this Society some of whom seldom appear in comons pay noe dutyes and decline the exercises of the house and others have taken military imployments upon them and others without gownes and with swords have in a tumultuous manner assembled themselves in the comon Hall . . . and in an irregular way encompassed the Bench and, by getting upon the cupboard and tables in the said Hall, loud acclamacons and by flinging upp their hatts did very much disturb the peace and infringe the ancient good government of this Society."[14] The occasion was the moving of an address of thanks to Charles for a declaration in April which had given reasons for the dissolution of the Fourth and Oxford Parliaments. Luttrell names Radcliffe as one of the "chief sticklers for the said address."[15] One of his fellow "loyal gentlemen" was Robert Fairbeard, to whom he had dedicated his *Ovid Travestie* in 1680.[16] After the activity of 1680, 1681, and 1682, when his collection, *The Ramble: An Anti-Heroick Poem. Together with Some Terrestrial Hymns and Carnal Ejaculations* was published, there is no more evidence of his contribution to the bustle of Restoration London. It could be that he did not long outlive his father, who died at his High Holbourn house 24 July 1682. Certainly Radcliffe was dead by the time that *Ovid Travestie* was reprinted for the 1696 *Works.*[17]

Radcliffe's elegy on Edward Story suggests that he probably belonged to an informal club of poets and wits presided over by Story, who was Principal of Barnard's Inn.[18] Here over glasses

14. *The Pension Book of Gray's Inn . . . 1569-1800*, ed. R. J. Fletcher, 2 vols. (London, 1901-10), II, 65.

15. *A Brief Historical Relation of State Affairs from September 1678 to April 1714*, 6 Vols. (Oxford, 1857), I, 99.

16. See Luttrell, loc. cit. . Fairbeard entered Gray's Inn the year before Radcliffe (25 April 1668) and was called to the Bar 5 August 1671 (see Foster, p. 304 and Fletcher, II, 16).

17. He is described as "late of Grayes Inn" in the Term Catalogues for November 1696 (*TC*, II, 606). For later references to Radcliffe, see *POAS*. . . . Vol. 6, pp. 165 and 179. Blackwell's Catalogue A10 (1980), p. 5 describes a copy of Fulke Greville's *Certain Learned and Elegant Works* (1633) bearing the signatures of Alex: Radcliffe and Helena Radcliffe. The latter signature probably marks the volume out as belonging to an Alexander from the Leigh branch of the Radcliffes (see Hampson, p. 299).

18. *Alumni Cantabrigienses*, ed. John and John A. Venn, 4 vols. (London 1922-27), and Foster, pp. 250 and 319.

of claret Radcliffe seems to have read his own and listened to others' poetry. Without suggesting that all his poetry was read to these gatherings, it may be said to express the taste of the "witty Club." First, Story's circle was as Tory as its claret drinking. Claret was popularly taken to symbolize loyalty, as opposed to coffee, the drink of the Whig and the seditious, but the polarization was more than political. Claret suggested a fine, gracious, and untroubled existence, whilst coffee brought with it the restlessness that attends activism. Radcliffe himself wrote of the distinction in his song "*To the Tune of* Per fas per nefas" in which wine is held to promote "true living" and to improve discourse, whereas coffee makes its drinkers' conversation "tedeous":

'Stead of Authors both learn'd and facetious,
They quote onely *Dugdale* and *Oats*.

There is more than a hint of Tory complacency in Radcliffe's song, of a grudging recognition of the threat posed by the Plot, and a myopic view of that threat as a thorn in the side of good living. Although the Club listened to political songs "of Bloody Plots against the Throne/And Government," and although Radcliffe himself composed "The Lawyer's Demurrer" in response to the fracas at Gray's Inn in 1681, wit and civilised living took priority over politics. The risqué, the scurrilous, the iconoclastic, and the "learn'd and facetious" are all elements of Radcliffe's poetry which play to the audience of Story's group or their like. A few translations apart, his verse projects the bearing of a loyal and witty gentleman: it is rakishly familiar, occasional, and above all it often enjoys a witty irreverence, seen in a restrained form in the elegy on John Sprat as well as in the anti-heroic "The Ramble." It is an irreverence which can spill over on to normally sacrosanct subjects. In the anti-Danby song "Thomas did once make my heart full glad" it overflows into an ironic monologue spoken by Charles which reflects adversely upon his easiness. In the final stanza Charles laments:

I gave him all Christian Liberty,
I let him sometimes lig by me,
I let him feel my Duchesses Knee,
Yet *Thomas* I fear has betray'd my Realm.

Despite this flash of disrespect Radcliffe remains in essence a Tory. He should not be confused with his uncle, Robert, also a captain, who was to throw in his lot with Monmouth. And he must be distinguished sharply from Rochester because for all the burlesque elements of Radcliffe's poetry it lacks the sceptical energy which informed Rochester's accounts of contemporary politics and society and pushed him towards a Whig stance in the last three years of his life. The irreverent wit of Radcliffe's verse often indulges as much as it ridicules its subject.

Rochester shares with Byron the claim to be the most irreverent poet in the English language, but his irreverence is inseparable from his scepticism. The distinction between his sceptical disrespect and Radcliffe's much simpler irreverence is important. The first is highly personal, the second the dialect of a tribe; the one is exploratory, the other uses wit to keep questions at bay. Whereas for all its detachment Rochester's "Satire against Reason and Mankind" expresses the personal, sceptical dilemma of a man poised between two conflicting sets of values, [19] Radcliffe's pseudo-philosophical poem "As Concerning Man" expresses a more formulaic disillusionment. The form and content of Rochester's "Satire" show him to share Montaigne's concern to see two (or more) sides to a question without Montaigne's saving fideism; Radcliffe's stated perplexity is dissipated by his poem's cavalier ending, which removes the poem from the realm of personal expression and turns it into a fashionable pretence at disillusionment:

'Twere better then that Man had never been
Than thus to be perplex'd: *God save the Queen*.

This distinction needs to be borne in mind when we focus on Radcliffe's burlesques, the work for which he is best remembered. Restoration burlesque is often thought of as linked with some form of scepticism—it has recently been suggested, for example, that the large number of lyrical parodies in the later seventeenth century grows out of a Montaigne-like emphasis on the relativity of viewpoints[20]—but although Radcliffe's burlesque parodies of "several late songs" assume a different per-

19. See K. E. Robinson, "Rochester's Dilemma," *DUJ*, LXXI (1979), 223-31.

20. Jeremy Treglown, "Scepticism and Parody in the Restoration," *MLR*, LXXV (1980), 18-47, esp. 18f. Treglown's equation of scepticism with viewing from a different perspective broadens the term so much as to limit severely its usefulness.

spective, the effect is not sceptical. Once again it helps to imagine Radcliffe addressing himself to the audience represented by Story's club, his poems savoured for their "learn'd and facetious" wit. If they substitute one attitude for another (normally the realistic for the idealistic), they never put two attitudes in tension. They have more of the status of a witty man-of-the-worldly retort than of a thought-out alternative. In Radcliffe's burlesque of the song "Now, now the fight . . ." from Lee's *Theodosius* the retort replaces a song of blissful sexual unity with one of sexual conflict which builds to a climax of male bravado and an exhortation to drink.[21] Radcliffe might have capitalized on a note of threatened imperfect enjoyment in the model, but he preferred a version which asserts male self-sufficiency. This was much more in keeping with the motto from Mantuanus quoted on the titlepage of *The Ramble:* "*semel insanivimus omnes.*"[22] His retort is also critical. To be fashionable as a young Inns of Court man it was necessary to affect the critic. No doubt the members of Story's club sat "critic-like" at their meetings as well as in the theatre pit. In his parody of Lee, Radcliffe was drawing attention to the sentimentality of Lee's song, but his policing of contemperary style is not confined to the burlesques of "several late songs." He snipes at Lee again in his account of contemporary writers in "News from Hell". Here he has his eye on the dramatist's heroic bombast, actualizing the bathetic mixture of the larger-than-life and the ordinary latent in a line from the end of Act IV of *Oedipus.* Lee's line runs:

> But Gods meet Gods, and justle in the dark:[23]

Radcliffe simply rearranges it so as to highlight the very unethereal word "justle":

> So, Gods meet Gods i'th'dark and justle.

21. For details of Lee's song, see Claude M. Simpson, *The British Broadside Ballad and Its Music* (New Brunswick, 1966), pp. 523-25. There is a convenient text in *The Penguin Book of Restoration Verse;* ed. Harold Love (Harmondsworth, 1968), p. 157f. Radcliffe also parodies "Hail to the Myrtle Shades" from *Theodosius,* II. ii.

22. Ecloga I, l.118. For references to Mantuanus in English literature, see *The Eclogues of Baptista Mantuanus,* ed. Wilfred P. Mustard (Baltimore, 1911), pp. 37-52.

23. John Dryden and Nathaniel Lee, *Oedipus* (London, 1679), p. 65.

In a poem such as Samuel Butler's "Elephant in the Moon" this reduction of the affected by reference to the ordinary can be part of a sceptical method, but here Radcliffe comes close to enjoying the telling collocation for its own comic sake. In his *Ovid Travestie,* however, where his burlesque art is seen to best effect, he exploits the ordinary to very different purpose.

When Dryden's collection of translations of Ovid's heroic epistles appeared in 1680, it prompted a burlesque by Matthew Stevenson (?), *The Wits Paraphras'd: Or Paraphrase upon Paraphrase,* which in turn prompted Radcliffe's *Ovid Travestie.*[24] In his preface Dryden stresses the naturalism of Ovid's epistles, but not without reservation, confessing "that the Copiousness of his Wit was such, that he often writ too pointedly for his Subject, and made his persons speak more Eloquently than the violence of their Passion would admit."[25] Radcliffe set out to reduce this eloquence and to render the epistles' expressions of emotion both more natural and more ordinary. On occasion the result can be strikingly original. One such occasion is the version of the epistle from Canace to Macareus. Radcliffe's Canace is no longer hyper-eloquent, but very ordinary, not very intelligent, and not very articulate. She undergoes the same passionate disturbance as Ovid's Canace, the painful throes of an incestuous love gone wrong, but her reactions are different. The marriage of relative inarticulacy with emotional anguish has both tragic and comic potential. Radcliffe's verse hovers between the movingly simple utterance which we associate with Mistress Quickly's account of Falstaff's death and the comic artlessness of Jonas Dock in *The What Do You Call It.* The effect is set up at the outset of the poem:

> Before these rude, distracted Lines you read,
> Believe the unlucky Authress of 'em dead.

24. Dryden's *Ovid* was advertized 6 February 1679/80 in the *Protestant (Domestick) Intelligencer,* and *The Wits Paraphras'd* appears in the Term Catalogues for May 1680 (*TC,* I, 394). From the epistle from Hypsipyle to Jason, dated 27 February 1679/80, it seems that Radcliffe began his travesties before Stevenson's (?) volume was in print. They were not, however, published until the autumn, by Jacob Tonson (Dryden's publisher), who operated from Gray's Inn Gate. An expanded edition appeared in 1681.

25. *The Poems of John Dryden,* ed. James Kinsley, 4 vols. (Oxford, 1958), I, 180.

Ever to see me more's beyond all Hope,
One hand a Pen, the other holds a Rope:

This opening places Radcliffe's version between the grandeur of Dryden's

If streaming blood my fatal Letter stain
Imagine, e're you read, the Writer slain:
One hand the Sword, and one the Pen employs,
And in my lap the ready paper lyes.[26]

and the cheap bawdy of *The Wits Paraphras'd:*

If menstruous Bloud can make a spot
Imagine I am gone to pot.
One hand employs my Pen, alas!
With t'other hand I scratch my A . . . .[27]

By the end of the fourth line a note of bathos has begun to sound with the substitution of a rope for Ovid's and Dryden's sword, and in the next couplet the poetry sinks:

My blustring Father's troubled with a Whim,
And I must hang my self to humour him.

The note of burlesque reduction in "blustering", the comic rhyme, and the disproportion between Aeolus's known anger and Canace's expression of it combine to make it seem that comedy has arrived to stay, but with the new paragraph the verse shifts back into a more sympathetically expressive mode:

But when he sees my Carcase on the floor,
Surely he'll cease to call me Bitch or Whore:

It is difficult to know whether to laugh or to be sympathetic, to be disrespectful or respectful. This disquiet pervades the whole epistle. Canace suffers too much to be comic, but she is too comic to be heroic. She is the commonplace reality. By operating on the boundaries between irreverence and the heartfelt Radcliffe can both pose questions about the proper style for natural expressions of emotion and engage sympathetically (but not sentimentally) with the perspective of an unheroic Canace. In so doing he transcends the surface irreverence of *The Ramble* and shakes free of any simple comparison with Rochester. The travesties of Ovid need to be considered alongside Butler's or Cotton's burlesques, for although they do not share the optimis-

26. Kinsley, I, 187.
27. *The Wits Paraphras'd* (London, 1680), p. 9.

tic Baconian scepticism underlying Butler's burlesque method or the fleeting hints in *Scarronides* at the importance of simple country values as an alternative to the epic, they do at their best get beyond a merely negative opposition of the ordinary to the high-flown.

Temperament as well as historical accident no doubt helped to determine the tone of Radcliffe's poetry, but it has been useful to see the verse of *The Ramble* as an expression of the taste of his immediate milieu, not just as the verse of "a Gray's Inn wit" but as that of one of a group of loyal and witty gentlemen of Gray's Inn. Unlike Rochester's, it is the poetry of a type rather than the poetry of an individual. *Ovid Travestie* is an extension of the art of this more occasional poetry. It is still "learn'd and facetious," but it marks the emergence of an individual burlesque voice. It is no surprise that, unlike *The Ramble,* the travesties of Ovid passed into several editions.

THE TEXT

The 1696 *Works* is made up of the third edition of *Ovid Travestie* (1696) and the first edition of *The Ramble* (1682), with a new general titlepage. The third edition of *Ovid Travestie,* which was advertized separately from the *Works (TC,* II, 606), is a reprinting of the second and augmented edition of 1681. The present text is a facsimile of a copy of the 1696 *Works* in the Library of the University of Newcastle upon Tyne by kind permission of the Librarian.

Ken Robinson

The University of Newcastle Upon Tyne

THE
WORKS
OF
Capt. *ALEX. RADCLIFFE*
In one Volume.

VIZ.

Ovid's *Traveſtie: Or a Burleſque upon* Ovid's *Epiſtles*.

Likewiſe his Ramble, an Anti-Heroick Poem, with ſeveral Miſcellanies.

The Third Edition Augmented.

LONDON,

Printed for *Richard Wellington*, at the *Lute* in St *Paul*'s Church-Yard. MDCXCVI.

TO

ROBERT FAIRBEARD OF GRAYS-INN, *Esquire.*

SIR,

HAving committed these Epistles to the Press, *I was horribly put to't for a Patron—I thought of some great Lord, or some Angelique Lady; but then again consider'd I should never be able to adorn my Dedication with benign Beams, coruscant Rays, and the Devil and all of Influence. At last I heard my*

A 2 good

good Friend Mr. Fairbeard *was come to Town--nay then---all's well enough. To you therefore I offer this English* Ovid, *to whom you may not be unaptly compar'd in several parcels of your Life and Conversation, only with this exceptiou, That you have nothing of his* Tristibus *you.*

'Tis you who Burlesque all the Foppery and conceited Gravity of the Age. I remember yon once told a grave affected Advocate, That he Burlesqu'd God's Image, for God had made him after his own Likeness, but he made himself look like an Ass.

Upon

Upon the whole matter I am very well satisfi'd in my Choice of you for my Judge; if you speak well of the Book, 'tis all I desire, and the Bookseller *will have reason to rejoyce: tho' by your appaobation you may draw upon your self a grand Inconvenience; for perhaps you may too often have Songs, Sonets, Madrigals, and an innumerable Army of Stanza's obtruded upon you by*

Sir,

Octob, 28*th*. 1680

Your humble Servant,

Alex. Radcliffe.

TO THE READER.

Occasioned by the

PREFACE

To a late Book call'd

The WITS Paraphras'd.

BEfore I shall give you any Account of our Old Friend *Ovid*, or of his *Life*, I am to inform you, that his *Epistles* have been ingeniously and correctly translated by several Gentlemen; and withall, that he was of a good Family, and a brave Fellow was he.

Now,

Now, ſince the unhappy Accident of his Death, his Ghoſt has been lately attempted to be rais'd by an unlucky *Pretender* to *Poetry*, who indeed hath not skill enough to diſturb his Manes: He calls his Book, *The Wits Paraphras'd*, or, *Paraphraſe upon Paraphraſe*, that is, *Throw, Pelion upon Oſſa, Oſſa upon Pelion, and away with it.* This Book he has dedicated to his Patron *Julian*, Secretary to the Muſes, in hopes that he may get and Under Writers Place ſomewhere about *Pernaſſus*: but alas! how can he ever hope for Preferment, when he has blaſpheam'd the beſt *Poets* of our Age, by miſtaking *Innocence* for *Ignorance*: I wiſh to God the laſt may not riſe up in Judgment againſt him. He (good Soul) is (as appears in his Epiſtle to his Patron) for none of your High Flights, but, like an humble Sinner in a ſtrict Diet, makes all his *Similies* of *Cloofe-Stools* with *Velvet-Seats*, and *Pans* that receive the Excrement. God ſave us: What are we when we are left to our ſelves.

Now

Now for his *Preface*, he would imitate that ingenious one of Mr. *Dryden*'s to *Ovid*'s *Epistles*, in beginning with *Ovid*'s Life, which hath been wrote by as many Men as there is *Lives* in *Plutarch*. And again, our *Paraphraser* saies, That *Ovid* was as good a Wit as Himself, or any other Translator; and, to prove that, he saies, *Nescivit quod bene cessit*, &c. He might as aptly have said,

The Man in the Moon drinks Claret.

Then he saies, That he could find no such thing as *Clubbing* with *Ovid* in all the Catalogue of *Virgil*, *Catullus*, *Propertius* or *Tibullus*: very truly said: for I suppose he knows nothing farther of those Authors than the Catalogue.

Oh Tempor! Oh Mores!
The more the merrier!

He

He wonders, that ſo many Workmen ſhould put their Shreds and Thrums together to deſs *Ovid* in a *Buffoon*'s Coat! why a ſilly *Quaker*, in plain *Taunton* Serge, thinks a Scarlet Coat embroider'd to be the *Old Serpent*!

He queſtions not but that there are more Fools in the World of his Opinion. (The true Queſtion is, whether he is not ſingle?)

Then he affirms, that, in his own ſimple naked ſhape, he comes nearer the Original, than the beſt of 'em; when in *Sapho* to *Phaon* he begins at the ſixth Diſtich, *Arva Phaon celebrat*, &c. and goes back to the fith, *Uror ut in Domitis*, &c. leaving out the eight Verſes preceeding, by which you may eaſily gueſs that he had no other Authority for his *Paraphraſe* (as he calls it) than the Tranſlation: Tis ſomething ſtrange, that neither *Ovid* himſelf, nor Ninteen Judicious Tranſlators, can give this Gentleman the leaſt hint or light into *Publius Ovidius Naſo*'s meaning.

Quo

Quo te mori pedes?——

Now on a ſudden he's ſtarted from Poetry, and is poſſeſt with the Spirit of ſublunary Wealth, and wiſhes with all his heart that he were as rich as a *M.* or a *C.* then would he quit all his title to P*ernaſſus*, and engage never to write: oh, never to write any more, that is to ſay, he'd be ſo unconſcionable as to have a good Eſtate for nothing:

God proſpor long our Noble King——

Now, as he ſaies, the late Tranſlators have already clipp'd the Original, and why ſhould not he clip too: whereas my fear is, he hath clipp'd *Ovid* ſo cloſe that it will hardly go:

When firſt King Henry, *&c.*

I

To the Reader.

I believe no Book hath had ſeverer uſage than our *Paraphraſers*; for ſaies he, it was hurry'd into the Preſs before it cou'd make any defence for it ſelf: Now the meaning on't is, if it had met with impartial Judges, it had never been Printed.

The Glories of our Birth and State, &c.

But to conclude; Having wonderfully ſhew'd his Reading in his Preface to his aforeſaid *VVits Paraphras'd*; in Scraps of old *Latin*; and at laſt, to his eternal Glory, one bit of falſe *Greek*; he is ſo far encourag'd, that he gives any man a Challenge in *Chaldee*, *Arabick*, and *Syriack*, though he confeſſes he knows nothing of the matter: But, to try him, I'll leave him with this S*yriack* Hexamiter.

Erytit ut ælutap ſnabucer bus enimget igaf.

And

And to let you know that this laſt Verſe, though ſomething rough, is not the effect of Indignation, I part friendly; only with this Advice, That our *Paraphraſer* would conſider, and follow any other Employment, more agreeable with his Genius (if he have any) then that of Poetry.

THE

THE TABLE.

Sapho to *Phaon*, Pag. 1.

Phillis to *Demophoon*, p. 2

Hypermnestra to *Linus*, p. 16

Hermione to *Orestes*, p. 22

Canace to *Macareus*, p. 28

Ariadne to Theseus, p. 37

Leander to *Hero*, p. 45

Hero's Answer, p. 54

Laodamia to *Protesilaus*, p. 60

Oenone to *Paris*, p. 69

Penelope to *Ulysses*, p. 78

Phædra to *Hypolitus*, p. 85

Hypsiphile to *Jason*, p. 95

Paris to *Hellen*, p 105

Hellen to *Paris*. p. 119

SAPHO

SAPHO to PHAON:

The ARGUMENT.

Sapho *was a Lady very Eminent for Singing of Ballads, and upon an a extraordinary Pinch, could make one well enough for her Purpose: She held a League with one* Phaon, *who was her Companion and Partner in the* Chorus , *but* Phaon *deserted his Consert for the Preferment of a Rubber in the* Ba'nnio. Sapho *took this so to heart, that she threatens to break her Neck out of a Garret Window; which if effected, might prove her utter Destruction. Authors have not agreed concerning the execution of her Design: But however she Writes him this loving and terrifying Epistle.*

When these my doggrel Rhimes you chance (to see,
You hardly will believe they came from (me,
Till you discover *Sapho*'s Name at bottom,
You'l not imagine who it is that wrote 'em.

I, that have often Sung—*Young* Phaon *strove*,
Now Sing this doleful Tune— *Farewel my Love*;
I must not Sing new Jiggs---the more's the Pity,
But must take up with some old Mournful Ditty.
You in the *Bannio* have a place, I hear;
I in my Garret Sweat as much, with Fear:
You can rub out a Living well enough,
My Rent's unpaid, poor *Sapho* must rub off;
My Voice is crack't, and now I only houl,
And cannot hit a Treble for my Soul:
My Ballads lye neglected on a Shelf,
I cannot bear the Burthen by my self;
Doll Price the Hawker offers very fair,
She'l Sing along with me for Quarter-share;
Sue Smith, the very same will undertake,
Their Voice is like the winding of a Jack.
Hang'em, I long to bear a Part with you,
I love to Sing, and look upon you too;

Besides,

Besides, you know when Songs grow out of fashion;
That I can make a Ballad on occasion.
I'am not very Beautiful,——God knows;
Yet you should value one that can Compose:
Despise me not, though I'm a little Dowdy,
I can do that---same---like a bigger Body:
Perhaps you'l say I've but a tawny Skin;
What then? you know my Metal's good within.
What if my Shoulder's higher then my Head?
I've heard you say I'm Shape enough a-Bed:
The Mayor (God bless him) or the worthy Sheriffs
Do very often meet with homely Wives.
Our Master too; that little scrubbed Draper,
Has he not got a Lady that's a Strapper?
If you will have a Beauty, or have none,
Phaon must lye----*Phaon* must lye alone:
I can remember, 'fore my Voice was broke,
How much in praise of me you often spoke,

And when I ſhook a Trill, you ſhook your Ears,
And ſwore I Sung like, what d'ee call'em--Spheres;
You kiſs'd me hard, and call'd me Charming witch,
I can't do't now, if you wou'd kiſs my Breach.
Then you not only lik'd my airy Voice,
But in my Fleſhly part you did Rejoice;
And when you claſp'd me in your brawny clutches,
You ſwore I mov'd my Body like a Dutches;
You clap'd my Buttocks, o're and o're agen,
I can't believe that I was crooked then.
Beware of him you Siſters of the quill,
That Sing at *Smithfeld-Bars*, or *Saffron-Hill*,
Who, for an honeſt Living, tear your Throat;
If *Phaon* drinks w'ye you're not worth a groat:
And Ladies know, 'twill be a very hard thing
To ſink from him the ſmalleſt Copper-farthing;
Avoid him all —— for he has us'd me ſo,
Wou'd make your hearts ake, if you did but know,

My

My Hair's about my Ears, as I'm a Sinner,
He has not left me worth a Hood or Pinner.
Phaon by me unworthily has dealt,
Has got my Ring,----though 'twas but Copper gilt;
Yet that vexes me,----Th' ungrateful Pimp
Has ſtole away my Peticoat with Gimp;
Has all my Things, but had he left me any
I can't go out alone to get a Penny
Phaon I ſhould have had leſs cauſe to grieve,
If like a Man of Sence, you'd taken leave:
That you'd be gone, had I been ne'r ſo certain,
We might have drank a Pot or two at parting;
Or fry'd ſome Bacon with an Egg; or if
Into ſome Steaks, we'd cut a pound of Beef,
And laugh'd a while, that had been ſomething like;
But to ſteal off, was but a ſneaking Trick.
My Landlady can tell, how I was troubled,
When I perceiv'd my ſelf ſo plainly bubbled:

I ran like mad out at the Alley-Gate
To overtake you but it was too late:
When I confider'd I had loft my Coat,
If I had had a Knife I'd cut my Throat;
Yet notwithftanding all the ills you did,
I Dream of you as foon as I'm in Bed;
You tickle me, and cry, Do'ft like it *Saff*?
Oh wonderous well! and then methinks I laugh.
Sometimes we mingle Legs, and Arms, and Thighs;
Sometimes between the fheets, methinks does rife:
But when I wake and find my Dream's in vain,
I turn to fleep only to Dream again.
When I am up, I walk about my Garret
And talk I know not what----juft like a Parrot.
I move about the Room from Bed to Chair,
And have no Satifactoin any where.
The laft time I remember you lay here,
We both were dry ith' Night, and went for Beer;

Into

Into the Cellar by good luck we got,
What we did there, I'm ſure you ha'n't forgot:
There ſtands, you know, an antiquated Tub,
'Gainſt which, ſince that, I often ſtand and rub;
Only to ſee't, as much delight I take
As if the Veſſel now were full of Sack;
But more to add unto my Diſcontent,
There's been no Drink ith' Celler ſince you went.
There's nothing but affords me Miſery,
My Linet in the Cage, I fear will dye:
The Bird is juſt like me in every thing;
Like me it pines Like me it cannot Sing.
Now *Phaon*, pray take notice what I ſay,
If you don't bring the things you took away;
You know my Garret is four Stories high;
From thence I'll leap, and in the Streets I'll die:
May be you will refuſe to come----Do--- do,
Y' had beſt let *Sapho* break her Neck for you.

Your afflicted Conſort, Sapho.

PHILLIS to DEMOPHOON:

The ARGUMENT.

Demophoon *was born in* Holland, *who took after his Father* Theseus, *pretending to the Art of Pyracy, he was cast upon* Newcastle-Shore *by adverse Winds* (*as the* Dutch *Commentators say*) *but we are inform'd he came hither by his own choice. No sooner arriv'd, but he heard that one* Phillis, *a single Woman, kept an Inn in the Town; There he took up his Quarters:* Phillis *observed him as a lusty Younker, and though his outward Habiliments were not very tempting; yet his person perswaded her so far, that she Married him, and entrusted him with all. After some time, he told his Wife that his Occasions call'd him into* Holland *to see his Father, who he said, was a Man of mighty Substance; He promised to Return within a Month, but hath not been heard of since. Therefore she writes to him this Letter; but whether it came to his hands or no, hath been a question to this day.*

YOur absence does discover your Disdain,
You've done enough to make a stone complain;

You

You told me you wou'd ſtay a Month,---no more;
But by my Nature I do find 'tis four.
I, who am Woman, and a Lover too,
Obſerve the change of Moons, much more than you:
Indiſpoſition in the Head, or Back,
Informs our Sex beyond an Almanack.
Sometimes I hop'd---but ſoon that Hope did ſink;
Sometimes I thought---I knew not what to think.
I made my--ſelf a Liar———notwithſtanding
There was no Ship--I ſwore I ſaw you Landing.
Some Curſes on your Father I beſtow,
That old *Dutch* Rogue, think I, won't let him go:
But then again, that cannot likely ſeem,
The Maggot bites---you're gone away from him;
What if you ſhould be wrack't when hither bound?
No,--you're to great a Villian to be down'd.
Whom ſhall I blame? whom but thy ſelf---fond (*Philly*?
Who haſt liv'd now Thirty years, and art ſo ſilly.

When

When first you did within my Doors set footing,
I fell in Love--forsooth--A Pox of rutting;
The Devil sure will have that Doctor *Hymen*,
Who told me, that his business was to try--men:
He did believe--you'd prove an honest Man,
Marry'em said he, with all the speed you can;
The Good old Man his Substance to increase,
Would match a Hellhound to a Saint for Fees:
You swore such dreadful Oaths as ne'r was heard,
By th' *Belgick* Lyon, and the Pirnce's Beard;
By *Opdam*'s Ghost, and by the Dragon's Tail,
B' your Father's Head, and Mother's Farthingale;
By the great Cannons, and the Bloody Flag,
And by the *Hogan Mogans* of the *Hague*,
Your execrations put m' in such a fright,
That all the Hair about me stood upright:
If on your Head these Curses fall you've nam'd,
I must conclude, that certainly y'are damn'd;

Hearing

Hearing ſuch bloody Oaths, you would not ſtay,
I made all haſte I could to get y'away;
I furniſhed you with all I cou'd afford,
Bisket and Powder'd Beef I put aboard;
A Flask of Brandy to your girdle hung,
Better I'm ſure, was never tipt o're Tongue:
And when I pach'd your Sails with antient Smock,
I thought they wou'd have brought me home (good luck;
But ſtead of that---ſuch was my Fatal Hap,
I prov'd the Inſtrument of your Eſcape:
When you came hither in a low Condition,
Did I not ſtuff your Gut with good Proviſion:
The Suit y' had on---was deſtitute of ſtitches.
I gave you then my Brother's Coat and Breeches;
But as for that---Pox on't--- I'll ne'r repent it,
What you had wanted, I had then preſented;
If you had never paid---here's none would ſtop ye;
But I muſt be your Wife too ----like a Puppy:

I wiſh to God that very day we met,
That into Gaol I had been thrown for Debt:
Then if I'd ask'd the Queſtion ——you'd have ſaid
Thank you, forſooth, I'm not in haſte to Wed.
Well, well! Myn Hier! y've caught me now 'tis true,
I hope I am the laſt you will undoe.
The *Dutch* by Paint deſcribe each others Lives,
And draw their Neighbours Actions, and their (Wives;
They'l draw your Father as ſome petty Pirate,
Doing ſmall things, which People wont admire at.
He has been Rogue enough, but done no Wonders,
'Has rob'd a Fiſherman, of Eels and Flounders:
Perhaps he's Drawn making a Sailor drunk,
Diving in's Pockets——to equip his Punk;
Theſe are but Trifles to what you have done,
The Father's but a Coxcomb---to the Son:
You ſhall be Drawn, firſt in your tatter'd Cloaths,
Humbly complaining, full of Lies and Oaths;

And

And then you ſhall be Rigg'd from head to foot,
And from your Mouth, this Label ſhall come out;
"Poor *Phillis*, of *Newcaſtle* upon *Tyne*——
"'Twas I that ruin'd---now you ſee, I'm fine.
What muſt I do? I have not Trading here,
And all my Neighbours do but laugh and fleer;
One cryes, Where is your Husband *Demo*——foe?
For your right Name, not one of 'em does know;
Another cryes out---Hey! for *Amſterdam*;
What! Was'a *Dutchman* Phillis---or a Sham?
Thus (as they ſay) they throw you in my Diſh;
Wou'd I cou'd have you here but with a wiſh,
For theſe Rogues ſake; 'twould be good ſport to ſee
How well you wou'd belabour two or three;
Then they'd change Tone, and cry---God bleſs ye (both,
You are a handſom Couple, by my Troth:
No---'tis in vain to hope that you'l return,
I muſt continue, as I am their ſcorn;

But

But yet I can't forget the parting Day,
I thought you wou'd have hugg'd your Breath away;
At laſt you ſpoke--'twas this confounded Lye,
Phil, in a Month this o're again we'll try;
But I believe that trick you're trying now
With ſome tun-belly'd *Rotterdam*——*V'froe*:
If *Phillis* ſhou'd be talk'd on by the *Dutch*,
You'l ſay you never heard of any ſuch.
Phillis! Who's ſhe? Where does this *Phillis* dwell?
If you don't know, *Demophoon*, I'll tell;
"This is *Newcaſtle-Phillis*, ſhe that did
"Once entertain you, Sir, at Board and Bed.
"Some ſmall Remembrance *Phillis* hath deſerv'd,
"Had not this *Phillis* been, you might have ſtarv'd
"She gave you Money, like a fooliſh Elf;
"At laſt this *Phillis* gave away her---Self.
I am that *Phillis*, if I had my due,
That ſhou'd have Hang'd my ſelf for Loving you:

It will not be too late to do it ſtill,
And if I'm in a humour, 'faith I will.
Then on my Grave let theſe few lines be writ,
Which *Phillis* made her-ſelf in Moody fit.

Here Phillis *lyes,*
Had ſhe been wiſe,
S'had Wed a Neighb'ring Scotchman;
And then ſhe might,
Have liv'd in ſpite
Of any Drunken Dutchman.

HYPERM-

HYPERMNESTRA to LINUS.

The ARGUMENT.

There was lately a Gang of English *Highway-men, all of 'em having Wives or Whores in* London. *Now the only means to detect 'em, was by bribing their Women. In order to which the Keeper of* Newgate *went to 'em all, promising them very fairly, and with all, using Arguments how serviceable they wou'd be to their Country, in Discovering them; which they might easily do, when they came home to Bed. The Women were easily perswaded, And one Night, order'd the Keeper to be there at such a time, who seized them all; but* Linus *was praeadmonished by his Wife* Hypermnestra, *so he escaped away in her Cloaths; She bore the brunt in his Apparrel, and was Taken (supposed to be a man) and Committed to* Newgate, *and put into Irons. The rest of the Thieves were Hang'd, her Tryal was respited, being not known who she was.* Hypermnestra sends *him this Letter.*

TO thee poor *Hypermnestra* now complains,
Such is the Torture of my Iron Chains
Shall it be call'd in Law, a Crime so heinous,
For being just to my own Husband *Linus*?

Let

Let 'em torment me on, I do not care,
I'll not tell who I am, nor where you are.
If they ſhou'd Hang me up inſtead of you,
To the laſt Gaſp I ſwear I will be true:
I long to be reveng'd on tyoſe curs'd Wives,
That did betray their Friends and Husbands Lives.
Such Men were not in *England* to be found,
They'd bid the Devil ſtand, on any ground;
And all the prizes that they got, they ſpent
Upon thoſe Whores; yet they were not content,
Think on that Night we did together Sup,
When all the Company were Cock-a-hoop;
That fatal Night you all came from the Pad,
Your Booty very large, your hearts were glad:
Though in my ſad Condition, 'tis not proper;
Yet, I can well remember all the Supper:
A ſtately Loin of Veal began the Feaſt,
I help'd you half the Kidney at the leaſt;

Four Turkey Poulets came next you wiſh'd they'd (been
Four *Turkey* Merchants upon *Mile-End-Green*;
Roaſted young Ducks, and Chickens fricazeed;
There was more meat than we cou'd eat indeed:
Wine in abundance---I drank none but Sack,
But all you men did ply it with Pontack:
To th' top you fill'd a Glaſs, and drank to th' beſt---
The Health as you began it, ſeem'd a Jeſt;
I took't in Earneſt to my ſelf, and knew
That I ſhou'd prove the beſt of Wives to you.
By Two a Clock you Men were almoſt Drunk,
Then each to bed went to his Spouſe or Punk;
If they were all as kind as you to me,
Never was ſuch a Night of Lechery:
At laſt you ſleep ſecurely without warning
Of the ſtrange Alterations in the Morning:
I knew betimes the Keepers wou'd be there,
And all the Night I ſweat, 'tween Sport and Fear

At last I rose, and 'bout the Room I walk'd,
And thus at Randum to my self I talk'd;
Have I not sworn a Thousand Oaths at lest,
That I'd betray my Husband with the rest?
What must I do? 'Tis true, I am his Wife,
What! must I damn my Soul to save his Life?
Hang all the Oaths in Christendom, said I;
He is my Husband, and he must not die.
With that I drew your Breeches on in hast,
The Codpiece was so big, I was amaz'd;
I walk'd into your Coat, hanging on Peg.
I lost my head within your Perewig:
Having put on your Armour Cap-a-pee,
For by the weight, such was your Cloaths to me,
You reach'd your Arm across---had I been there,
You would have had the other bout, I fear;
I pull'd the Sheet and Blanket from the Bed,
I plainly then perceiv'd, 'twas as I said:

Riſe *Linus*, Riſe, ſaid I, be very quick;
This is no time for any wanton Trick;
You're all betray'd——The Conſtable's at Door,
You muſt not ſtay a minute of an hour.
I ſhuffled on my Cloaths upon your back,
They did not fit—I heard my *Manteau* crack:
No ſooner were you gone, but in they bounc'd;
They ſeiz'd on me, and ſwore I ſhou'd be trounc'd.
And here they have me faſt with Bolt and Lock;
They know not yet that I have on a Smock.
Now you are ſafe, and I am here, dear *Linus*
Let's ſeriouſly diſcourſe th' Affair between us:
If all the truh to them I ſhould diſcover,
What can they ſay? 'twas acted like a like Lover
I may be ſent to *Bridewel*, there they'l bang me;
But all the Law in *England* cannot hang me.
While I lye here—I am in little eaſe,
But when all's told, what ſhall I do for Fees?

If

If you don't uſe ſome means to get me freed,
Within few days you'l hear that I am Dead;
And then 'tis like they'l bury me; if ſo
Upon my Grave this Epitaph beſtow:

Here lies a Wiſe, who rather than ſhe'ld fail
To ſave her Husband's Life, dy'd in a Jayl:
My Irons load me ſo, I'm fit to cry,
I would write more, but cannot; ſo God b'ye.

HYPERM-

HERMIONE to ORESTES:

The ARGUMENT.

Hermione *was the Daughter of* Menelaus *and* Hellen. *Her Mother ran away with a young Fellow, one* Paris, *they went together beyond the Seas. Her Husband who lov'd her well, persu'd 'em, and after many years, found his Wife and rescu'd her from her Gallant, and without any resentment of the Injury, took her again. During their absence, their Daughter (who had an Estate left her by her Unkle) was committed to the Custody of her Grand-father, who marri'd her to a School-fellow and Cozen German of hers, by name* Orestes. *Her Father brought home with him one* Pyrrhus *a wild young Fellow, to whom he Marri'd her again, taking no notice of the first match. She silly harmless Girl, wonders at the design, and to her Husband* Orestes *writes this innocent Letter.*

TO thee I write my dear and only Cuz;
Nor will I be afraid to call thee Spouse:
Though here's a Fellow come resolv'd to swear
I am his Wife, and he will mak't appear:

He

He looks sometimes, as if he long'd to eat me,
Sometimes he looks so gruff, as if he'd beat me:
He says he is *Achilles* Son and Heir,
And bids me disobey him, if I dare;
He kisses me so hard, the strongest man,
He gets a top of me do what I can;
With all my strength my Legs together joyn,
But with one Knee, hee'l open both of mine.
I call him Rogue and Rascal, filthy Sot,
And all the beastly Names I can get out:
I'm Marry'd Sirrah, therefore don't mistake it,
I have a Husband that will thwack your Jacket:
Yet that's all one, he cares not what is said;
But by the Hair he drags me into bed:
They talk of Girls, forc'd by unruly men,
They can't be forc'd so much as I have been:
Yet all this while *Orestes* comes not near me,
I am afraid you do not love your *Hermey*;

 You'l

You'l fight for Money, as you'd fight for Life,
And won't you fight a little for your Wife?
On while my Father mist my Mother *Hellen*,
Lord ! There was such a noise,and such a yelling,
He rais'd up all the People in our Lane,
And ne'r was quiet, till she came again.
I wou'd not have you make a noise for me,
But come and kill this fellow quietly ;
Give him a good sound blow, and never fear man,
It is for me, your Wife and Cozin German.
You know my Guardian marri'd me to you
When we were both so young, we could not do---
Now from beyond Sea comes my Father huffing,
And will needs marry me to this same Ruffian,
He vapours here about his Country Blood,
I guess your *English* Familie's as good :
He says, you've led a very wicked life,
And that you broke your Mothers heart with grief.

For

For talking ſo of you, I'd ſlit his Tongue,
And pull his Eyes out too, if I were ſtrong;
'Tis ſomething ſtrange, we're of a Generation
Where Raviſhing has been a mighty faſhion:
My Grandmother was raviſh'd by one *Swan*,
A little Couzin by another man;
My mother has been raviſh'd once or twice,
And I am raviſh'd now by her advice.
Muſt I with ſuch a Rogue as this be match'd?
A more unlucky Girle was never hatch'd.
My mother left me here a little Wench,
Juſt big enough to clamber on a Bench;
She was ſtark mad for that young fellow---*Paris*,
And after him ſhe danc'd the new Fagaries:
My Father for his life cou'd not forbear,
But ran a--catter-wawling after her;
Now they're come home, but with ſuch alt'red (looks,
As if they ſome were ſtrange Outlandiſh fo'kes.

My

My Father has a Beard below his Band,
I did not know my Mother, ſhe's ſo tann'd :
Toward my good, what did ſhe ever do ?
When ſhe was gone, I larn't to knit and ſow ;
I uſe my needle now as well's another,
But 'tis no God-a-mercy to my Mother :
When ſhe came in, ſhe knew not who I was ;
This Girl, ſaid ſhe, is grown a ſtrapping Laſs,
She muſt be marry'd or ſhe'l grow too buſie ;
(Huſſy :
Look here, I have brought thee home a Husband,
With that he threw his Paws about my Neck ;
Kill him, *Oreſtes*, or my heart will break :
I draw the Curtains when he's faſt aſleep,
And out of Bed, ſoon as 'tis day, I leap ;
But I do toſs and tumble all Night long,
As if by Bugs and Piſmires I'd been ſtung :
Sometimes when I'm aſleep, by chance there lies,
(thighs ;
One of my hands ſqueez'd cloſe between his

I

I ſnatch't away as ſoon as e're I wake,
With as much ſpeed, as if I'd felt a Snake;
To th' other ſide o'th' Bed, I jerk from him,
And ſometimes lay one Breech upon the Beam;
Then after me, he by degrees will ſteal,
Pray Sir keep off, ſay I, I am not well;
He ſeems as if he did not underſtand,
And then he reches out his haſty hand;
I ſpeak as plainly to him as I can,
I tell him I'm not fitting for a Man.
Pſhaw, Pſhaw! ſays he, I know you do but jeſt.
'Pon the whole matter he's a filthy Beaſt:
For God's ſake *Orey*, Prethee-now contrive,
Some way or other that he may not live:
For here I take my Oath upon a Book,
If you don't get me off by hook or crook,
That we may do as marry'd People my,
I'll either kill my ſelf, or run away.

CANACE to *MACAREUS*: Lately tranſlated out of OVID Now BURLESQU'D.

The ARGUMENT.

Macareus *and* Canace, *Son and Daughter of* Æolus (*a Trumpeter of the Guards*) *being from children brought up together, at the laſt grew ſo intimately acquainted, that they made bold to lie with one another.* Canace *prov'd with Child by her Brother* Macareus. *She was deliver'd in the houſe; and the Nurſe contriv'd to convey the Child through the Hall when* Æolus *was ſounding his Trumpet, accompany'd with ſeveral ſorts of Wind-muſick; notwithſtanding that noiſe, the ſhrill Cry of the Infant was over-heard by* Æolus, *who ſent it away to be left in the Streets, and expos'd to the mercy of the Pariſh; and to his Daughter* Canace *he ſent a* *Hal-*

Halter, with this Message, ---This you have deserved, ----and you know how to use it. Canace *hang'd her self (as you may guess) before she wrote this Letter.*

BEfore these rude, distracted Lines you read,
Believe the unlucky Authress of 'em dead.
Ever to see me more's beyond all Hope,
One hand a Pen, the other holds a Rope:
My blustring Father's troubled with a Whim,
And I must hang my self to humour him.
But when he sees my Carcase on the floor,
Surely he'll cease to call me Bitch or Whore:
His puffing and his blowing will be in vain,
He cannot puffe me into life again:
His Mind is swell'd much bigger then his Face,
I am (he saies) his Family's Disgrace:
All his great Friends and Kindred are provok't;
What are his Friends to me when I am choak'd?

I

I wiſh that we had ſtifled one another
That night I clung ſo cloſely to you, Brother:
Why did you love me more then did become ye?
It had been happy, if y'ad kick'd me from ye:
When firſt, with pleaſure, I lay under you,
Would y'ad been lighter by a ſtone or two.
  At firſt I wondred what ſhould be the matter,
I look'd like Death, and was as week as Water:
For ſeveral days I loath'd the ſight of Meat,
And every night I chew'd the upper Sheet:
I'd ſuch Obſtructions, I was almoſt moap'd,
My Breath came ſhort, my —— were ſtop'd.
  I call'd old Nurſe, and told her how it was;
She, an experienc'd Bawd, ſoon groap'd the Cauſe:
Quoth ſhe, for this Diſeaſe, take what you can,
You'll ne'er be well, till you have taken Man:
When I was young, I thought I was bewitch'd,
I ſcrach't my Belly, for it alwaies itch'd.

The

The Truth I will no longer hide, ſaid I,
I muſt enjoy my Brother, or I die:
She tickl'd me, and told me 'twas no Sin,
Nearer of Blood, ſaid ſhe, the deeper in:
Both you and I approv'd what Nurſe had ſaid,
So, without more a-do, we went to Bed:
You in my belly rummag'd all about,
To find this wonderfull diſtemper out:
Too ſoon 'twould be diſcovered, was my Fear,
I could have let you ſearc'd for ever there:
But Nurſe can tell how I did ſigh and ſob
When we perceiv'd that you had done the Jobb.
I made th' old Beldam foot it up and down
To every Quack and Mountebank in Town,
For *Dendelion*, and *Camelions-thighs*,
Spirit of Saffron mixt with *Vulters-eyes*:
I would have given all I had been worth,
T' have kill'd the Child, before it had come forth:

But

But the ſtronge Rogue lay fencing in my Womb,
And did thoſe pois'nous Potions overcome:
Oh! when I ſaw the ninth Moon in the Wane,
Then I was in the Full----of grief and Pain;
Then, then my Throws came on m thick and (thick;
I groan'd but for my Life I durſt not ſchreik
Untill my Tortures came to ſuch a growth
That Nurſe with both her Hands did ſtop my (Mouth:
I ſhould have cry'd ſo loud, that every Neighbour
Would have diſcover'd I had been in Labour:
No woman yet that ever wore a Navel,
Endur'd ſo hard and ſo ſevere a Travel.
I curs'd your Sex, and wiſh'd a Rot might come
On all the Stallions throughtout Chriſtendome,
At laſt you came; I knew you by your tread;
I peep'd at you, though I was almoſt dead:

T'ward

T'ward me you ſeem'd to have ſome kind Re- (morſe
But look'd, as if you would have eaten Nurſe.
  You held my back-parts, you could do no more;
Would you had never felt the Parts before.
  Siſter, ſaid you, you ſhall not die this bout,
We're both unluky, but, we'll rub it out.
  To ſee what words from thoſe we love can do,
(*Surely* the Child within me heard you too,)
For ſtreight he ſprang forth from me, and did ſeem
To make his paſſage in a flowing Stream:
'Twas hard enough: but now's a harder Caſe,
To hide the Buſineſs from my Father's face;
We did conſult how to deviſe a way
Thorough the Hall our Baſtard to conveigh.
  My Father in Wind-muſick ſtill delighted,
And all the Gang that night he had envited:
Fellows that play on Bag-pipes, and the Fife;
The old man always lov'd a noiſeful Life:

They all did ſound together after Supper,
And then to carry 'em off, we thought, was proper.
  Nurſe, in her Apron took the little Brat,
Swath'd up in Linnin, Ruſhes over that;
Quite through the Hall ſhe went her uſual pace,
And, unconcern'd her ſelf, humm'd *Chevy-Chaſe.*
  Juſt to the door s'had ſafely carry'd him,
When the unlucky Wretch began to ſcreme:
His little Organ made a ſhriller noiſe
Than all the Fluits, Recorders, or Ho-boies:
The old man prick'd his ears up, like a Hare,
And after Nurſe ran nimbly, as the Air:
Whither ſo faſt, ſaid he, old Mother Trundle?
Pray, let us ſee, what have you in your Bundle:
Quoth Nurſe,—'Tis Mriſtreſs *Canny's* dirty Smoak,
Men into Womens ſecerts ſhould not look.
  He puff'd away the Ruſhes from her Lap,
And there appear'd the little ſprauling Ape:

'Zound's

Zounds, saies my Father, What is here? A Kid!
My Daughter *Canny*'s finely brought to bed?
He rais'd so great a Tempest in the House,
I thought that Hell it self was broken loose;
He rag'd so loud, the Bed shook under me;
Methought I was in some great Storm at Sea:
He rush'd into the Room, and did discover
The bloody Symptoms of a Child-bed Lover:
Our Sexes Stains by him were here discry'd
Which Women from their own dear Husbands (hide:
With his own hands he did design to wound me,
But that he saw something like Murther round me:
The Bastard in the Streets he did expose,
And what will be his destiny, God knows:
The little Knave, with Tears, did seem to answer,
As who should say, I beg your pardon Gransir,
Out went old *Trump*; I by his Looks could find
There was some mischief hatching in his mind,

D 2 In

In came a Fellow of the *Bag-pipe* Gang
Whose very Whiskers seem'd to say, go hang;
Before his words came out his tongue did falter;
At last he spake, *Canny*, look here's a Halter:
Your Father saies, 'Tis this you do deserve;
If you'll not use it, you may live and starve.
His most obedient Daughter he shall think me;
If I don't hang my self, the Devil-sink me.
Since Whoreing does produce such strange effects
Would I'd been born a Monster without Sex:
Let my young Sisters all be warn'd by me,
And curb betimes Incestuous Lechery.
This I request of you, Dear Brother *Mac*.
That of our wretched Child some care you'd take;
If you can find him out, be not unwilling,
Towards his maintenance, to drop a shilling.
Let these my last words be observ'd by you,
As I obey my Father's: ——so, —Adieu.

A R I-

ARIADNE to *THESEUS*, Lately tranſlated out of OVID Now BURLESQU'D.

The ARGUMENT.

Theſeus, *an Engliſh Gentleman, and one who for his diverſion admir'd Travelling,* eſpecially on Foot, *having ſafely arriv'd at* Calais, *walk'd on eaſily from thence to* Paris, *where he had not long been but he receiv'd an unmannerly Juſtle from a Cavalier of* France: Theſeus, *whoſe great Soul could not brook the leaſt Affront, reſented this ſo highly, that he challeng'd him, fought him, and after a long and skilful Diſpute between 'em, fairly kill'd him:* Theſeus *was impriſon'd in the* Baſtile; *During his Reſtraint he held a League with* Ariadne, *the Keeper's daughter: And, though the Priſon was as difficult as a Labyrinth, (ſuch is the power of Love,) ſhe*

she soon contriv'd a way for his Escape by night: and he, accompany'd with Mistress Ariadne, *footed it back to* Calais; *where, both lodging together at the* Red-Hart, *he very unkindly took the advantage of her Snoaring, and stole from her early in the morning; and went off with the Pacquet-boat to* Dover; *from whence he gently walk'd to* London: Ariadne *sends him These.*

NO savage Bear, no *Lyon*, *Wolf*, or *Tyger*,
Would ever use his Mistress with such (Rigor;
D'ye think you don't deserve ten thousand Curses,
For leaving me in Pawn at Monsieur *Forces*?
I wonder what the Tavern-people think!
For here I sit, and dare not call for Drink.
While by your side I innocently lay,
You might have taken leave, a civil way:
I was half waken'd from a pleasant Sleep
By th' melancholly sound of *Chimney-sweep*:
I stretch'd my Leg, to find out my Bed-fellow,
But I could groap out nothing but the Pillow:

Thinking

Thinking t' have hugg'd you in my Arms ſo cloſe
One of the Bed-ſtaffs almoſt broke my Noſe:
Theſ. Theſ. ſaid I, I hope you are not gone:
I might as well have call'd the Man i'th' Moon:
I rent my Head-cloaths off, *mortdieu*! *mordieu*!
What will become of me? What ſhall I do?
I op'd the Caſement as the Morning dawn'd;
And could plainly ſee that I was pawn'd,
With calling you I tore my Throat to pieces,
The Eccho jeer'd me with the name of *Theſeus*:
To th' top of all the houſe I ran undreſt;
The people thought that I had been poſſeſs'd:
At laſt, I ſpy'd you in the Pacquet-boat;
I knew it was you or ſo at leaſt I thought:
Had you been walking, I had known your Stride,
And gueſs'd your Strutt from all Mankind's beſide:
Both Seas and Winds muſt needs be kind to thee
Thou art ſo like 'em in Inconſtancy.

I thump my Breaſt, I rage, I ſtorm and fume;
The Houſe deſires I would diſcharge my Room:
Quoth one o'th' Servants, Miſtreſs *Ariadne*'s
Paſt all recovery, overwhelm'd with Madneſs:
Another crys, *Mam'ſell Com' portez vou'?*
Fetch me my *Theſ.* ſaid I, What's that to you.
When in the Boat I cou'd no longer ſee you,
Ten thouſand De'ills of Hell, ſaid I, go we' you.
  They think I'm drunk, I'm ſure'tis not with (Wine;
The Score's too large; and you have left no Coin.
Into a Corner I am ſometimes dogg'd,
And there I cry as if I had been flogg'd:
Sometimes I roul my Self upon the Bed,
And act thoſe poſtures o're that once we did:
To my own ſelf with pleaſure I repeat,
Here lay my Head, and there I put my Feet:
I often call to mind our amorous Work;
Then here, methinks I have you with a Jerk.

Some-

Sometime they talk, that Ships are ſafe at home:
I liſten then, to hear if you are come.
Were I a Man, into the Seas I'd douſe,
And after you I'd ſwim, and bilk the houſe:
If I ſhould offer to run home again,
My Father 'd keep me in an Iron-chain;
I have betray 'd the old Man's Truſt for you;
I may go whiſtle for a Portion now:
When, for your ſake, I ſtole the Priſon Keys,
I little thought to ſee ſuch days as theſe:
Oh! when your L O V E was mounted to a pitch,
You hugg'd me as the Devil hugg'd the Witch;
You ſwore, with Oaths moſt deſperate and bloody,
The Queen of *France* to me was but a Dowdy.
I have more Whymſes then a dancing *Bear*,
Sometimes I dream the Conſtable is here:
And though the Waiters very often wheedle,
Yet I ſuſpect that they will bring the Beadle.

Again,

Again, I fear they'll ſpirit me away,
And ſend me Slave into *Virginia* :
I was not bred a Drudge from the beginning,
Except it were to waſh my Fathers Linnen.
Either to Sea or Land I durſt not look,
To Heav'n I can't; you've ſtole my Prayer-book:
Your Valour made my Fortune ſo untoward,
I would to God that you had been a Coward:
Diſtreſſed *Ariadne* now complains,
Becauſe ſuch ſprightly blood runs in her Veins :
They ſay we *French* are very Hot, 'tis true;
But yet our Sparks are Froſt and Snow to you:
Curſt be the time when you firſt learnt to fence,
(Though that does never alter Men of ſence.)
I fancie in what poſture you were found,
One Foot heav'd up, the other on the Ground:
As much of Warlike Grace you did diſcover
As any *Roman* Statue in the *Loure*.

Methinks

Methinks I hear you ſpeak to th' Cavilier,
Sa ! *Sa* ! *Monſieur*, I have you here and there :
But now your valiant Acts are loſt for ever,
By ſneaking off, like a *French-Ribbon-Weaver*.
Had I not drank that *Brandy* over night,
I cou'd have wak'd, and ſo have ſtop'd your Flight.
Curſt be the Wind which was ſo kind to you ;
Curſt be the Boat, and curſt be all its Crew ;
Curſt may I be for truſting what you ſaid ;
Curſt may all Lovers be that Snore in Bed.
Poor *Ariadne*, thou art finely ſerv'd,
Thy too much Love has brought the to be ſtarv'd:
The Servants pitty me, and ſay't's a hard caſe,
I've nothing here to pay 'em with but Carcaſe :
This Carcaſe too has wept out all its Juice,
'Tis grown ſo dry, 'tis fit for no Man's uſe.
Think, when you're rev'ling in your Cups at *London*,
That your Poor *Ariadne* here, is undone,

And

And when you come where people do resort,
To hear your Travels told were pritty sport:
With what tough bit of Flesh you did engage;
You thought you should be killing him an Age:
Do not forget me when you tell your Tale,
Tell'em how I releas'd y'out of Goal;
And how with you I stole on foot through Allys;
And, pray forget not, that I am pawn'd at *Callais*:
And, when this Tale to your Companion's told,
Imagine *Ariadne* stiff and cold:
When dead, they'll bury me in some back Garden,
For I can't give the Parish-Clerk a farthing.
And 'tis for you I all those Sorrows prove;
So, Mr. *Theseus*, thank you for your Love.

LEANDER to HERO:

The ARGUMENT.

Leander *an Usher of a School, and chief Poet of* Richmond, *having contracted a more then ordinary Acquaintance with Mistress* Hero *of* Twitnam, *a Governess or Tutress to young Ladies; such a reverential esteem had they procur'd to themselves at each place, that they could not conveniently meet without great scandal; therefore the Usher frequently swam over to his Mistress by night, but at this time the* Thames *was so rough, that he was constrained to convey his mind to* Hero *by a Waterman in these Poetical Lines, wherein Love and Learning strive to outvie each other.*

YOur faithful Lover sends this Bille' dou'x.
Stuff'd full of Love, but not a word of news.
Believe not, I think much of any Labour,
Cou'd I have come my self, I'd ne're sent Paper;
The *Thames* is rough, the Winds so hard do blow,
I scarcely got a Waterman to go.

And if I wou'd have given a thousand pound,
This was the only Fellow to be found.
I stood upon the Shoar, while he went off,
The Boat once gone, I thought 'twas well enough.
I must be careful whom I send by Water,
Our Family begins to smoak the matter:
Just as the Letter went, I had a fancy
Came in my head, I cou'd have made a Stanza :
Go Paper, go, and kiss a whiter hand,
That oft hath put *Leander* to a stand.
Methinks, the Nymph perfumes it with her Breath,
And bites the wax of with her Ivory Teeth:
Her Sheperd would be glad to be so bit,
Untill th' aforesaid Teeth together met.
But then think I, these whymses shee'll condemn.
The hand that writes, should rather make me swim;
Bold strokes in Poetry she hardly blames,
But such bold stroaks shou'd be upon the Thames:

Methinks

Methinks it is an Age ſince I ſwam o're,
I long untill each Arm, does prove an Oar.
Fully reſolv'd I came to'th water ſide,
And thought the ſpace between us but a ſtride.
I ſaw your houſe, and wiſh'd that I cou'd clamber
To your watch--- light in the ſupremeſt Chamber:
I pull'd off Coat and doublet twice or thrice,
But then I thought,--- be merry and be wiſe.
Thus I in Verſe ſpake to the mighty *Boreas*,
Thou bluſtring youth——pray tell me why ſo fu-(rious;
Tho' amongſt Winds thou art a great Commander,
Blow gently for the ſake of poor *Leander*.
I croſs no Sea (Here *Thames* is call'd the Sea,
Becauſe it doth with lofty Verſe agree.)
I croſs no Sea to *Aſia* or to *Afrique*,
Upon the Account of Sublunary Traffique:
Ingots of Gold! alas! I do not ſeek 'em,
Give me my Heroes Love, then *omnia mecum*.

Boreas

Boreas himſelf does ſometimes leave off roaring
And goes a—woing, I'll not ſay a--whoring.
For ſeveral uſes you, your breath may ſpare,
Do not ſo fiercely move our *Richmond* Air.
But all was vain, *Boreas* was ſtill unkind,
I did repeat my Verſes to the wind.
Had I but wings, I'd ſoar above the People
And place my ſelf juſt now on *Twitnam* Steeple.
I well remember that firſt night I ſwam,
That happy night I firſt to *Twitnam* came;
I put of all my cloaths, with them my fears,
And dous'd into the *Thames* o're head and ears.
The Moon took---care *Leander* ſhould not ſink,
And ſtole before me like a lighted Link:
I thank'd her for her Love, and thus did greet her,
As far as my poor Talent went---in meeter.
Ah gentle Moon, becauſe thou'rt kind to me,
I wiſh *Endymion* may be ſo to thee:

And

And as with him thou hold'ſt a private League
With thy broad Eye, ſo wink at my Intrigue.
Under correction to your Heavenly ſence,
Your caſe and mine have little difference.
A Goddeſs you love one of human Birth,
My Miſtreſs is a Goddeſs upon Earth:
Such ſort of Beauty as ſhe wears, is given
Only to ſuch as do belong to Heaven.
And if you are not of the ſelf ſame mind,
Begging your Pardon, *Cynthia*, you're blind.
With ſuch like words I got near *Twitnam* ſands,
And nothing all the way ſaw I but Swans.
At laſt I ſpy'd your Candle on the top,
Aye! now all's well, thought I, there is ſome hope.
But when you put your head out from the Caze-ment,
Then was *Leander* ſtruck into amazement;
For two Lights more did from the Window ſeem,
Which made the artificial one look dim.

Your Eyes the Moon, and Candle made juſt four ;
I, like ſome Prince was lighted to the ſhoar.
But you're to blame, when you perceiv'd me come,
Nurſe ſayes, ſhe cou'd not keep you in the room
But in your ſhift you wou'd be running down;
You'l get ſome violent cold, and then you're gone.
But to ſay truth, thou art a loving Tit,
Thou hug'ſt me in thy arms all dripping wet:
I can but think how ſtraingly I did look,
When you put o're my head a Holland Smock;
And hand in hand thus walking from the *Thames*,
We ſeem'd the Ghoſts of two diſtreſſed Dames.
But when we came to Bed, we underſtood,
We were no Ghoſts, but real Fleſh and Blood:
We did repeat more pleaſures in one hour,
Than ſome dull Lovers do in forty ſcore ;
Becauſe we knew our time was very ſhort,
We cou'd not tell the number of our ſport.

Auror.

Aurora does from *Tithon*'s Bed eſcape,
Tithon perhaps will take the other nap,
See her Poſtillian *Lucifer* before,
And now the Bus'neſs of the Night is o're;
The day appears, *Leander* muſt be jogging,
And home agen among the Boyes a-flogging.
My well beloved *Amo* I forſake,
And to dull *Doceo* now I muſt go back.
And Subſtantive I'll always be to thee,
My pritty Verb *Deponent* thou ſhalt be.
If we were in conjuction day and night,
Leander would not prove a heteroclite:
In Grammer we make Noun to joyn with Noun,
Why ſhou'd not *Twitnam* joyn with *Richmond* (Town?
'Twou'd make one mad to think a fooliſh River,
Or any ſurly Winds ſhould Lovers ſever:
But hold *Leander*, let no Seas nor Wind
Diſturb the quiet Freehold of thy Mind.

When first I crost- -my thought the Fish did gaze,
The Salmon seem'd to peep upon my Face;
I could hear Boatmen call from Western Barge,
What Fish is that, my thinks 'tis very large,
They'd call me Porpus,and they'd jeer and flout me;
But now by th' name of Brother they salute me:
How d'ee says one; Good morrow t'other cryes;
I civilly return them, *Bona dies.*
The Fishermen that bobs all night for Eel,
Now sayes, Your Servant, Sir, I wish you well:
God send you safe on t'other side the Water,
I say unto him, *Salvus sis piscator.*
I hope those Halcyon Nights will soon return;
For want of 'em, does poor *Leander* mourn.
But if such storms in Summer time does hinder,
How shall I e're get to the in the Winter?
If I do venture in, and should be drown'd,
I hope by thee my Body will be found.

Thou'lt

Thoul'troul it up in Holland or in Bucram,
Then may I truly ſay---*mors mihi Lucrum.*
But let not this poſſeſs you I am dead,
A fooliſh whimſey came into my head,
We ſhall have many pleaſant Nights between us,
I'll come and hugg my *Hero ore-tenus.*
Pray put theſe Lines up ſafe, for fear you looſe 'em,
In that warm place where I would be, your Boſom:
And in a little time, diſpute it not,
I'll come and juſtifie what I have wrot:
For when the wheather changes I'll not fail ye,
And untill then thou ——*dulce decus Vale.*

HERO's *Answer*.

L*Eander*, thank you kindly for your Letter,
Though if y'ad come your ſelf it had been (better;
I cannot reſt, I know not what's the matter,
I'm all afire, to have you croſs the Water.
We Women when we've any thing to do,
Are ten times more deſirous of't than you;
Having diſmiſt your little Boyes from School,
You can walk out i'th' the Evening when 'tis cool;
You can divert your ſelf a hundred wayes,
I only ſtand upon the ſhoar and gaze:
You have a Green in which you bowl or bett,
And now and then three or four ſhillings get;
Or to the Tavern, when you pleaſe you go
And drink a Bottle with a Friend or ſo;

Whil

While I ſit moap'd---like a neglected Cat,
And now and then with old dry Nurſe I chat:
What's your opinion, Nurſe, and tell me truly,
D'ye think the Wind to Night will be unruly?
What will *Leander* come? or keep away?
'Faith I don't know, ſayes ſhe, 'tis like he may;
Such drouſie anſwers I do ſeldom miſs,
D'ye think I han't a bleſſed time of this?
Up to my Chamber, when 'tis Night, I get,
And in the Window is my Candle ſet;
Perhaps I read a Play, or ſome Romances,
I ſoon grow weary of ſuch Idles Fancies:
Then I peruſe your Letter o're again,
And more and more admire your learned ſtrain;
Then I ask Nurſes Judgment in the caſe,
But ſhe old Soul's, as dull as e're ſhe was;
I make her ſtand uprigh (there I miſtake,
She can't ſtand ſo---for ſh' as a huckle back)

I mean, I ſet her ſomewhere in the Room,
And ſhe's to act as if you juſt were come ;
My only Joy (ſay I) thou'rt welcome hither,
How didſt thou ſwim to me this ſtormy wheather ?
Speak, let me hear ſome Muſick from thy mouth,
Nurſe nods, and ſays---I'm pritty well forſooth :
Thus I beguile the time till Morning---peep,
Then I go into Bed and fall aſleep.
And there I do enjoy you in my dreams,
Spite of the Devil or the rougher Thames.
Methought I ſaw you come ſtark naked in,
Wet were your locks, and dropping was your Skin
I with an Apron rub'd you up and down,
And dry'd you from the toe unto the crown ;
Then preſently we hugg'd with ſuch a force,
I ſhook the Bed, and wak'd and ſtartled Nurſe ;
And finding it to be a Dream---no more,
I grew as melancholy as before.

If

If in a dream ſuch tickling Joyes appear,
Much pleaſanter 'twou'd be, if you were here;
I don't know what to think: you us'd to ſay,
Ten Thouſand Devils ſhould not ſtop your way:
Why ſhould the danger at this time be more?
The Wind blows hard, and ſo it did before;
But now I ſee which way 'tis like to drive,
A *Richmond* Wench as ſure as I'm alive;
Ah! ſay ye ſo? why then it is for her
This Storm is rais'd, *Leander* cannot ſtir.
But hang't that cannot be, I'm turn'd a fool,
Leander was and is an honeſt Soul:
As ſoon as I had ſaid theſe words of you,
The Candle burn't not as it us'd to do;
Sayes Nurſe, there is a ſtranger in the Light,
Maſter *Leander* will be here to Night;
With that ſhe took the Brandy bottle up,
And pull'd from thence a very hearty ſup,

Sayes

Sayes ſhe--if what I ſay ſhould prove untrue,
I wiſh this bleſſed draught may ne're go through;
Therefore let's ſee you hear to night dear *Nandy*,
Or elſe poor Nurſe muſt never more drink Brandy.
Perhaps you fancy you take double pains,
And make to great a treſpaſs on your Reins,
To ſwim ſo far as you have us'd to do,
And after that to pleaſe a Miſtreſs too;
Half of one half I'd eaſe you if I cou'd,
And meet you in the middle of the flood;
But from the latter ſervice never flinch,
I ſhould be loath to bait you half an inch;
But after all excuſing what I'ave ſaid,
Pray do not croſs the River hand o're head;
I dream't laſt night, I hope 'tis no ill Luck,
A Spaniel Dog was hunting of a Duck,
There were ſome reads which under Water grew,
And more, perhaps, than the poor Spaniel knew.

He

He was entangled there, and there was found,
I came to help him, but the Curr was drown'd.
I do not tell this dream to make you tardy,
But as a Caution not to be fool-hardy.
The Wind will soon be laid, the *Thames* be clear,
Then you may cross it, without wit or fear;
Make much of this, for if you fail me, then
By all the Gods I'll never write agen.

LAODAMIA to *PROTESILAUS*, Lately Translated out of OVID: Now BURLESQU'D.

The ARGUMENT.

In the War between England *and* Holland, *one* Protesilaus, *an* English *Lieutenant of a Fifth Rate Frigat, being Wind-bound upon the* Downs; *his Wife* Laodamia, *hearing he was not gone off, sent him this Letter; and, like a fond Wife, gives him strict Caution to avoid Fighting.*

A Health to your Prosperity goes round,
And to your safe return before you're (drown'd:
My Neigybour *Jackson's* Wife began it to me;
If I don't wish it, may it ne'er go through me:

We

We drink, and fancie to our ſelves in vain,
That the good Winds will blow him back again.
I hate the noiſe of a tumultuous Sea,
Give me a Tempeſt rais'd by you and me;
A Storm in which all Parts about us ſhake,
When we can hear the Bed beneath us crack.
At *Graveſend*, when we took our laſt Adieu,
The Parting Kiſs, remember, I gave you:
I, like a ſhitten Girle, began to cry;
I had no mind, methoughts, to ſay, God b'w'y:
I heard Tarpaulins roar out, Hoiſe up Sail;
On Board, on Board; here comes a merry Gale:
In ſuch brisk Gales poor Women don't delight,
They blow away the pleaſures of the night:
As you went off, I could not bear the Loſs,
A Qualm came o'er my Stomach quite-a-croſs:
Old Mother *Crump*, a very ſubtile *Croan*,
Saw by my Looks that I was almoſt gone:

A Pint

A Pint of Brandy presently ſhe brought,
And made me drink a very hearty draught ;
She ſhew'd her Love, but what great good has't (done?
How can I live with comfort now you're gone?
I wake, and find no Husband by my ſide ;
I often think 'twere better I had dy'd :
Till you return, I'll ne'er be dreſt agen ;
I have not comb'd my head the Lord knows when:
A Glaſs of Wine ſometimes my heart does cheriſh ;
Wer't not for that, I fanſie I ſhou'd periſh :
Becauſe I go ſo taudry, like a Punk,
Some, that don't know me, think that I am drunk:
My Neighbours often tell me, Miſtreſs *Proteſ*----,
You go ſo ſtrangely, all the Street takes notice !
Says one, You do your Husband's Friends diſgrace ;
For ſhame ! Put on a Peticoat with Lace :
Why ſhould they think that I would wear a lac'd- (coat ?
When my poor Husband's in a Seaman's waſtcoat?

Should

Should I adorn my Head with curles and Towers?
When a poor Skippers Cap does cover yours.
The Plaguy *Dutch*; that they ſhould break the (Peace,
And not ſubmit to us in *Engliſh* Seas:
Though, for my own particular, I ſwear,
If I could once again but have you here,
Let *Dutch* have Liberty to fiſh and foul,
I would not care a Farthing, by my Soul.
Methinks I ſee you now, and, by your looks,
You are engaging with a Butter-box:
Methinks juſt now a Bullet did eſcape,
And hit my Neck, juſt in the very Nape.
But oh! I ſwoon, when I do think of *Trump*!
His Ships now giving yours a bloody Thump!
Bleſs us, ſaid I, Now, you are diſpatch'd!
That Dog has been at Sea 'fore you were hatch'd:
For Heaven's ſake avoid him if you can,
He's certainly the Devil of a Man!

If

If any Ship does make up towards you,
You may ſay ſure *Van-Trump*'s among the Crew:
There's not a Shot does to your Veſſel come,
But I receive the Pain on't here at home.
What am I better if you beat the *Dutch*,
And you come hither hopping on a Crutch?
How finely 'mong the Neighbourhood 'twou'd (ſhow,
To ſee you ſtrut upon a timber Toe?
To rout the Foe is ſome great Adm'ral's Office,
In theſe Engagements you are but a Novice:
Your ſingle Valours nothing on the Sea,
Your Combate ſhould be hand to hand with me.
Would I were in the Fleet with *Trump or Ruyter*,
To them I would becomean Humble Suitor,
And point out to them where your Squadron lay,
Directing them to ſhoot another way:
I'd ſpeak t'em thus; Great Souls of *Amſterdam*,
Pray hear a ſilly Woman, as I am;

And

And let your Cannon my poor Husband shun,
He knows not to discharge a little Gun:
If you were Women, as you're Warelike Men,
He would perform great Actions wi' you then:
Your Fighting, Skirmishing, and Breaking Bones,
Are only fit for Men that want their Stones.
Just as you were commanded to your Ship,
Remember, at the Stairs your Foot did slip;
Think on that Slip, and, when the *Dutch* are shoot-(ing,
Duck down your Head, as if you wanted footing;
I wish your Captain some good Coward were,
And durst not bring the Vessel up for fear:
I wish to God he would not sail too fast;
You'l come too soon, although you come the last.
When you return, they'll ask how matters stand;
I hope you'll know no more than we at Land.
All the day long I smell no sent but Powder,
Each minute Guns go louder off and louder.

Most marry'd women long till it be night,
But, for my part, I hate the thoughts of it;
Unless, by chance, I sleep, and dream of you:
Fancy's the kinder Husband then o'th' two:
And when I wake and feel the Linnen wet,
I find, I've wept for joy upon the Sheet:
This to Enjoyment gives but half content;
When shall we meet together by consent?
Oh, how I long to hear you tell in Bed
Some strange Romantick Tale of what you did!
But when you find you can't prolong the Jest,
And, being at *Stand*,--kiss out the rest.
 Against both Wind and Tide why will you go?
You'd scarce come home if Wind and tide said no.
You fight, methinks, about so mean a thing,
Which should have Privilege of catching *Ling*:
Old-Ling I hate worse than a Common Whore;
(Would you lov'd Fighting with the *Dutch* no (more:)

I ate

I ate it once, and that against my will,
And sometimes fancy that I smell on't still.
But though thou art expos'd to Seas and Wind,
It is some ease unto my troubled Mind
To see thy comely Picture in the Hall,
Drawn to the Life with Charcoal on the Wall:
I prattle to it as if thou wert here;
'Tis late; Pr'ythee let's go to Bed, my Dear:
Methinks thou say'st, I'll humour thee for once;
Thou'lt work me at the last to Skin and Bones:
I kiss the Wall and do my Ceeks besmear,
And ope my Mouth, as if your Tongue was there.
By all the pleasant Postures of Delight,
By all the Twines and Circles of the Night,
By the first minute of our Nuptial Joys,
When you put fairly for a Brace of Boys,

I do conjure you, have a ſpecial care,
And let not ſaucy Danger come to near;
For when I hear that thou art knock'd o'th' head,
I'll hold you ten to one that I am dead.

OENONE

OENONE to PARIS.

The ARGUMENT.

Paris *was the Son of* Priam *a Wealthy Old Citazen and Alderman of* London. *When* Hecuba *his Mother was big with Child of him, ſhe dream't a fooliſh conceited Dream, which occaſion'd Old* Priam *to conſult* Lilly, *who told him, That* Paris *in proceſs of time would occaſion his houſe to be burnt down. Therefore the credulous Alderman ſends him into the Country far* North *to be diſpos'd of as a By-blow. When he grew fit for Service he was entertain'd in a Gentleman's Houſe, where he contracted a Boſom-acquaintance with* Oenone *a Young Wench and fellow Servant with him in the ſame houſe. His Father began to come to himſelf, and hearing where he was, ſent for him, and own'd him as his Son; but before that, he had diſengaged himſelf from Service, and ran away with one* Hellen, *who was VVife to* Menelaus. Oenone *being inform'd of All theſe proceedings, writes to him this Letter.*

AFter my hearty Love to you remembr'd.
Hoping you are not in Body diſtemper'd,

More

More than my ſelf at the writing hereof;
If it be ſo, we are both well enough:
Your Uſage has been ſuch to poor *Oenone*,
That none but ſuch a fool as I would own'e'e;
I hear you're run away with *Menels* Wife,
I pitty her, ſhe'll lead a bleſſed Life;
What mighty miſchief have I done, I wonder;
You'l never have a younger, nor a ſounder.
If by my means y'had met with ſome diſaſter,
Had I procur'd you Anger from your Maſter;
If I had giv'n you that they call a Clap,
You'd had ſome ſmall Excuſe for your Eſcape:
But now you've had your ends, away to ſneak,
Come! come! theſe things would make a body, (ſpeak.
You were not then ſo Uppiſh---when you ſaid,
A Dutcheſs was a T—— t' a Servant Maid;
You were a Groom your ſelf, you know 'tis truth,
Not all your Greatneſs now — can ſtop my mouth;

If

If you were able to keep house you ſwore
You'd marry me for all I was your Whore.
We were together on a Summers day,
Both in the Stable, on a Truſs of Hay;
You can't forget ſome pretty paſtimes there,
No body ſaw us but the Cheſnut Mare:
You ſaid ſuch glorious things the very Beaſt
Prick'd up her Ears, and thought you were in Jeſt:
But I did prove th' verrier beſt o'th' two,
For like an Aſs I thought that all was true;
Soon after---you were taken from the Stable,
To wait upon your Maſter at his Table;
To undertake it you ſeem'd very loath,
Did I not teach you then to lay a Cloath?
There's no man but muſt have his firſt beginning,
Who learnt you then to fold your Table Linnen?
Did you not often when the Cloath were ſpread,
Juſt in the middle put your Salt and Bread?

You have been threatned oft to lose your place,
Because you knew not how to fill a Glass;
You pour'd in Wine up to the very top,
I told you you should fill but to the knob.
Did I not shew you how to broach your Drink,
And tilt the Vessel when't begin to sink ?
I was your dearest Honey---all that while
There was not such a Girle in Forty mile :
You carv'd my name upon the Trencher-Plates,
And on the Elms before the outward Gates ;
And as we see in time those Elms encrease,
So will my name grow greater with the Trees ;
And any one that stands but at the door,
May see *Oenone* (your obedient Whore.)
You never have been well, since those three Maids,
Rather those impudent and bold-fac'd Jades
Differ'd among them---selves, which it should be,
That had the cleanliest shap of all the Three.

To

To you they came when you were in the Cloſe,
The Little Field that was behind the Houſe,
Stark naked did they come from top to toe,
Paris, ſay they, we will be Judg'd by you.
Heavens preſerve you Eye-ſight---how you gaz'd,
Nor could you ſpeak a word, you were ſo maz'd ;
At laſt you Judg'd with many a hum ! and haw !
Venus the fineſt Wench that e're you ſaw.
This was a *Whitſon* Frolique, as they ſaid,
A pretty prank to ſhew you all they had.
To ſee how naked Women are bewitching,
Since that y'have minded nothing elſe but bitching.
Soon after that your project was of ſtealing
That over-ridden Whore that Miſtreſs *Hellen* :
I muſt be gone a little while, you ſaid,
(Then was this Bus'neſs brooding in your head.)
You kiſt me hard as if I cou'd not feel,
And ſwore that you wou'd be as true as ſteal :

Said

Said you---Doubt nothing, for the case is plain,
I'm proved the Son of an Old Alderman,
And sent for home my Father's very ill,
I must be by, at making of his will;
Oh that we cou'd but bury the old Cuff,
Then marry you, all wou'd be well enough.
You may've a richer Wife, but not a better,
For I am no such despicable Creature:
Not to disparage your good Lady Mother,
I can behave my self as well's another.
No Wife like me was there in Christendom,
When you were honest *Pall*---Squires *Sheepeard's* (Groom.
My Father's but a plain Old Man, 'tis true,
But's Daughter ha's been bred up as high as you.
He is an honest Man, whate'r I am,
And may be sav'd as soon as Master *Priam*.
Were I your Wife, my carriage shou'd not shame
Your Mother *Hec*.---tho' shee's a stately Dame.

What

What though these hands have us'd a Drippin-pan,
Yet on occasion they can furle a Fan.
Now on a little Folding Bed I lye,
(Tho' in that Bed sometimes lay you and I)
Yet I know how perhaps to hold my head,
If I were carried to a Damasque Bed.
If you had marry'd me y'had met with quiet,
What can y' expect from her but noise and riot?
You now have caught a most notorious Strumpet;
Besides 'tis known, as if y'ad blown a Trumpet;
Where e're you come you'l meet with frumps and (Jeers,
Her Husband too, will be about your Ears.
In little time from you she will be budging,
She'l lye with any body for a Lodging.
When first of all we closely were acquainted,
(Which now it is too late, I have repented)
Cassandra was a Gipsey in the Town,
Who went a Fortune-telling up and down;

I gave

I gave her broken meat, which we cou'd ſpare,
Shee'd tell me all my Fortune to a hair:
You love (ſayes ſhe) a Man not tall nor ſquat,
But a good hanſome Fellow, (mark ye that?)
This youth and you 'tis likely may do well,
If he eſcape but one----they call her *Nell.*
But if they two ſhould chance to lye together,
Hee'll break the heart of you, and of his Father.
Who this *Nell* was, I cou'd not chuſe but wonder;
But now I know who 'tis---a Pox confound her!
I'll make *Caſſandra* 'Liar tho', in part;
You've vex'd me, but you ne're ſhall break my (heart.
This very Whore I ſpack on, ran-away
With ſuch another Fellow t'other day,
And when her cloaths were gone, and money la-(viſh'd,
She came and told her Husband ſhe was raviſh'd.
I'm ſure I'm true, for here ſince you were gone,
Hath been ſome loving Boobyes of the Town,

One

One of the Fellows surely is a Satyr,
He follows me, and swears he'll watch my water:
We have a Servant come---pretends to Physick,
He hath a Cure for any one that-is-sick;
He cures the Tooth-ach; if your Finger's cut,
A Plaister to it presently hee'l put;
Freckles i'th' face he cures, and takes off Pimples,
'Hath taught me to the use of Herbs and Simples.
But I must beg my fellow-Servant's Pardon,
'Gainst Love there is no Herb nor Flow'r i'th (Garden:
For this Disease I must rely upon ye,
Come and live here again, you'l cure *Oenone*.

PENELOPE

PENELOPE to *ULYSSES*, Lately tranſlated out of OVID Now BURLESQU'D.

The ARGUMENT.

There hapning a Rebellion in Scotland, *in that Army which went under the Command of the Duke ;* Ulyſſes *went Voluntier. The Rebels being quell'd, the Army return'd home ; but* Ulyſſes *lay loitring at ſome Inn on the Road ; which when his Careful Wife* Penelope *underſtood, ſhe ſent him this Epiſtle ; giving him an Account how Affairs ſtood at home*

YOur poor *Penelope* admires that you
Should ever uſe a Woman as you do !

Now

Now every Soldier's at his own aboad,
You, like a Sot, lye tipling on the Road:
  You are not left behind 'em as a *Spy*,
T' inform, in case of second Mutiny:
The Devil of Hell will have that Fellow surely,
Who first began this Plaguy Hurly-burly,
Had it not been for this unlucky Fight,
Y'ad stuck to work all day :--- to me at night.
  Poor I must drudge at home all sorts of weather
And kit,---as Heaven and Earth would come together;
Twirling a Wheele, I sit at home--hum-drum,
And spit away my Nature on my Thumb:
Thus while I spin, you, like a carefull Spouse,
Go reeling up and down from to house.
Being you staid so long I did conjecture,
You had been maul'd by *Sauny*, the *Scotch* Hector:
Old *Nestor*'s Son, that Fool, stood just by you,
When's empty kcull, they say, was spilt in two:

And

And, when he dropt, for all you are so stout,
You wish'd your self at home, in shitten clout.
Yet after all, *Ulysses*, I am glad
You are a live, though you're a scurvy Lad.
Our Neighbours here all day do tittle tattle,
And talk of nothing else but Blood and Battle;
Were you at home, you could not chuse but laugh
To hear 'em crack and bounce, now they are safe:
Perhaps when three or four of them are met,
And round about a Kitchin-Table set,
there's such a Noise a Clutter, and a Din,
The Rebel *Scots* are routed o're agen.
Some with Tobacco-Pipes upon a Table,
Do valiantly demonstrate to the Rabble
The Foes chief Strength; with that another Spark
Hamilton's House describes; a third, the Park;
Another spils some Ale upon the Bench,
And, with his Finger, learns you to entrench;

One

One acts how fierce our valiant Soldiers ran on,
Diſmounts a Can, and tells you 'tis a Cannon;
Another cries Neighbours, obſerve and look,
This Pot's Sir *Thomas*, and this Glaſs the Duke.
Thus while the Husband draws this bloody Scheme,
The Wives, behind their Chairs, were in a Dream;
Nay, ſome of 'em (I queſtion whether 'ts true)
Do tell ſome mighty Deeds perform'd by you;
That, being provok'd, you like a valiant man drew,
And cut a *Scotch*-man's Luggs off by St. *Andrew.*
 I'm ne'er the nearer, though they're over-come;
If you'll not mind your Bus'neſs here at Home:
For my own part, I would not care a pinn
If they were ſtill in Arms, and you in mine:
Py'thee, come home; I cannot chuſe but wonder
What a God's-name you can be doing yonder:
By every Poſt and Carrier to the North
I've ſent more Paper than your Neck is worth:

I've ſent to *Hull*, to *Berwick*, and to *Grantham*;
I might as well have ſent a Poſt to *Bantam*.
Perhaps ſome Tapſter's Wife ſubdues your Heart,
Or elſe her Drink's ſo ſtrong you cannot part:
And, when you're drunk, Lord, how your Tongue does run,
That you've a Houſe well furniſh'd here in Town,
In which your Wife (or rather, Drudge) doth dwell
As conſtantly at home, as *Snail* in Shell.
(But yet, when I remember parting Kiſſes,
Then, then, methinks thou ſhouldſt be true, *Ulyſſes*.)
My Father ſays you're drow'd i'th watry Main;
The old Man joques, and bids me wed again;
His Counſel, like himſelf is ſtill unſound,
I'd rather he were hang'd than you were drown'd.
Every day here comes a ſort of Fellows,
Enow to make a fooliſh Husband jealous,
From *Whetſton*'s-Park, *Moor-fields*, or ſuch like places,
Fellows with Cuts and Frenches in their Faces;

There

There are but ſeven Fingers amongſt four,
And here they domineer, and ſwear, and roar:
Two of 'em ſay, they have been vaſt Commanders,
The other trail'd a Pike with you in *Flanders*;
There's one of 'em, they call him, Merry *Robert*,
He, in a merry way, broke up the Cubboard;
Here hath been *Irus* too, that *Iriſh* Thief,
W' hath eaten up a Surloin of Roaſt-Bief;
What ſignifies my Father or my ſelf,
We can't ſecure our Meat upon the Shelf?
What great defence can Nurſe or little Boy make
Againſt a Fellow with a Horſes ſtomach?
The little Rogue your Son, was almoſt drown'd,
Padling about he tumbled in the Pond,
But we recover'd him with much ado,
I hope he'll prove a better Man than you.
In ſhort, If ſpeedily you do not come,
You will be eaten out of houſe and home:

The old Man's crazy, we from him muſt part;
And I have lay'd your uſage ſo to heart,
That I am grown ſo wither'd now with Grief,
I look——more like your Mother than——

Your faithful Wife,

PENELOPE.

PHÆDRA

PHÆDRA to *HIPPOLYTUS.*

The ARGUMENT.

Theſeus *having made his Eſcape out of* France *with* Phædra——(*whoſe Siſter* Ariadne *he deſerted at* Calais) *when he came into* England *marry'd her, and brought her home to a Farm-Houſe near* Putney *in* Surrey, *which he Rented of one Mr.* Jove; *which Houſe during his Travell, (or rather his Ramble) he committed to his Son* Hippolytus, *who was a great Hunter, a hanſome Fellow, and a Woman---hater; for which two laſt Reaſons* Phædra *his Mother after ſhe had acquainted her ſelf with her Neighbours, and houſhold affairs, fell deſperately in Love; inſomuch that nothing would ſerve her but carnal copulation with her Son in-Law; to accompliſh which ſhe humbly entreats him by this Letter to conſider her Condition.*

TO you my Lad, I ſend this amorous Scroul,
Wiſhing you health, with all my Heart and (Soul;
Your Mother, and your Lover does beſeech,
That with theſe Lines you wou'd not wipe your (Breech:

Thank God, my Father gave his Children breed-
(ing,
And taught us all, our Writing and our Reading.
By Letters Men have News, and Women find
Which way and how their Sweet-hearts are en-
(clin'd.
Thrice I resolv'd to tell you all I thought,
But for my Blood I cou'd not get it out:
I just began to say——My dearest *Poll*,
Then laugh'd, and turn'd aside, and ruin'd all;
Tho' 'tis no laughing matter, for I own
I love the very Ground thou tread'st upon.
I'll tell thee, *Poll*, and mark me what I say,
If Love thou Sullenly dost disobey,
Tho' he's a Boy, not half so big as you,
Yet Fairy-like he'll pinch yo' black and blew;
On a full speed your Horse he'll lead astray,
And like a Hare he'll cross you in your way.
If he assaults—you cannot beat him him off
Either with hunting Pole or Quarter-Staff.

'Hath

'Hath ſworn, (tho' to your Father I am wed,)
To bind you faſt, and bring you to my Bed.
'Tis true, your ſtrength is great, his only Art,
You pitch the Bar, and he can throw a Dart,
What need I uſe theſe words? dear *Polly*—come
Let us embrace, your's not at home.
You know my Reputation's very great,
Whoo'd gueſs that You and I ſhou'd do the feat.
Oh how I am ſtung, I have as little Eaſe,
As if I had diſtrub'd a Hive of Bees.
I purre and purre, juſt like our Tabby Cat,
As if I knew not what I wou'd be at:
When Young, I cou'd have cur'd theſe am'rous (ſtings
With Carrots, Radiſhes, or ſuch like things;
Now there's no pleaſure in ſuch Earthly cures,
I muſt have things apply'd as warm as yours.
Where lies the blame, art thou not ſtrong, and (young?
Who wou'd not gather fruit that is well hung?

Or who ean call't a Sin when we have done,
Main't I have leave to hug my Husband's Son?
Suppoſe our Landlord *Jove*, that gallant Wight,
Had a months mind to lodge with me one night;
Nay——if his Lady too ſhould give conſent,
For you I'd quit him, though hee'd quit his rent.
Since you'l not hunt in this my ſofter place,
Where I ſhould get the better of the chaſe;
Since the large Fields and Woods you rummage, (through,
Disdaining my poor little Cunny——borough;
I'll follow you o're Ditches, and throu' Boggs,
And whoop and hollow after all the Dogs:
I'll ſpeak to th' hounds ſo well hey! *Jowler*, *Bow*. (*man*,
That none, but you ſhall know I am a Woman:
I'll praiſe your Greyhound *Dèlia*, when you courſe,
She ſhall my Miſtreſs be, and 'Ill be yours.
Under a hedge I'll ſquat down like a Hare,
And you alone ſhall find me ſitting there.

Some-

Sometimes upon a Horſe I'll get aſtride,
And after you, as I were mad I'll ride;
For all our Generation have been ſo,
When they're in Love they know not what they (do
You've heard that Miſtreſs *Europe* was my Gran- (dam;
She went away with *Jupiter* at Random.
Paſiphae my Mother was ſo full
Of ſtrange Vagaries that ſhe ſuck'd a Bull.
My Husband with my Siſter lay—or rather
I ſhould have told you it was your Father.
Poor *Adne* was ſtarke mad for him, and now
I am (God knows) as mad in Love with you.
So that between the Father and the Son,
There are two Siſters like to be undone.
I never ſhall forget with what a Grace
You dreſt your ſelf in order for the chaſe;
Your Viſage not too red, but only tan'd,
Of the ſame colour with your brawny hand.

An

An ancient Bever on your head you put,
Like a three——Pigeon Pye, in corners cut.
A little Jacket made of blewiſh green,
Which had the Death of many a Badger ſeen.
Your hair your own, which ſhew'd you not de-
(bauch'd,
Not nicely trim'd,for here and there 'twas notch'd.
I hate your Fellows with your powder'd Wigs,
As m' Husband us'd to ſay, they look like Prigs.
You'd laſting Breeches made of Buckskin Leather,
To keep the fundamental parts from weather.
But when you reach'd your hanger from the Bed,
Another Weapon came into my head.
Not all your days can give you ſuch delight,
Or half the Sport I'll ſhew you in a Night,
Delia's your Joy, *Delia* does you bewith ;
Can you neglect a Chriſtian, for a Bitch ?
Cephalus your Companion and old Crony,
Valu'd a Dog better than ready money.

Heed

Hee'd get upon a Horſe, though half aſleep,
Ready to hunt before the Day did peep;
But when h'ad once taſted *Aurora*'s ſweets,
He found out better Game between the ſheets;
For then unleſs ſhe pleas'd, he durſt not ſay,
(Nor did he wiſh) that it would e're be day.
Why ſhould not we conſent to try our skill?
I'm certain you and I can do as well.
Therefore dear *Poll*, I offer very fair,
Under *Barn-Elmes* I'll meet you if you dare;
Since none but Country Sports can humour you,
I'll wraſtle wi'll you there a fall or two;
Though o' my, Conſcience I believe you'l throw (me,
But if you ſhou'd, perhaps it won't undo me;
And when you have me down among the Trees,
You wanton Rogue, you may do what you pleaſe.
Wee'd no ſuch opportunity before:
Your Father is at *London* with his Whore.

There-

Therefore I think 'tis but a just design,
To cuckold him, and pay him in his coin.
Besides he ne're was marry'd to your Mother,
He first whor'd her, and then he took another.
What kindness or respect ought we to have
For such a Villain and perfidious Knave?
This should not trouble, but provoke us rather
With all the speed we can to lye together.
I am no kin to you, nor you to me,
They call it Incest but to terrifie.
Lovers Embraces are Lascivious Tricks,
'Mongst musty Puritans and Schismaticks.
Did not our Master *Jove* chuse him a Mistress,
Who should it be but one of his own Sisters?
There's no engendring can be truely good,
But when we fancy that we are of a blood.
Under the names of Mother and of Son,
What pretty pleasant actions may be done?

All they will ſay, becauſe I'm kind to thee,
I'm Mother both in Law and Equity:
Take heart of Grace, be not afraid of Spyes,
I care not if there were Ten thouſand Eyes;
I'll leave the door without the Bolt or Lock:
What if they ſaw us in our Shirt or Smock.
Nay I'll ſuppoſe we ſhould be ſeen in Bed,
What can there to our prejudice be ſaid?
That you came wet and dripping from the chaſe,
And I'd a mind to give you my warm place.
I did not think to've ſaid ſo much in haſt,
But Love like Murder muſt come out at laſt:
The Fort lies open, therefore ſcorn it not,
But come with ſpeed, and enter on the ſpot;
Let us imagine now the worſt can happen;
Suppoſe that you and I were taken napping;
And *Theſeus* ſays, Begone you filthy Whore;
Away you Rogue, and ſo he ſhuts the door.

What

What if he does, why then for *France* with ſpeed,
We ſhall be there ſupply'd with all we need.
My Father dwells at *Paris* in good credit,
And well to paſs is he, though I have ſaid it ;
There he's as well known as Begger knows his diſh,
We'll live as bravely then as Heart can wiſh :
Therefore make haſte, dream not of any harms,
Thou'lt be ſecure enough within my arms.
When you go out, may you be ſure of Game ;
May your horſe never tire nor happen lame :
At a default may the Dogs never be,
May *Delia* bring forth Whelps as good as ſhe.
May you i'th' Field ne're want a draught of Beer,
Or Bread and Cheeſe, or ſuch like hunting cheer.
While I ſit pining for you here at home,
When I have cry'd out both my Eyes you'l come.

HYPSIPYLE

HYPSIPYLE to *JASON.*

Lately Tranſlated out of

OVID:

Now BURLESQU'D.

The ARGUMENT.

Jaſon, *a* quondam *Foot-man, with ſome others, the nimbleſt of the ſame Function, joyn'd their Stocks, and purchas'd a Silver-Bowl, which they ran for from* Barnet *to St.* Albans; *but before the day of the Match, one* Medæa, *a Gipſey, and Strouler in thoſe Parts, took a more than ordinary fancy towards* Jaſon, *whom ſhe ſo dieted with new laid Eggs, or what the Devil it was elſe, (ſhe being ſuſpected of Witchcraft,) that he won the Plate; and beat two famous Foot-Jockeys,* Whipping-Tom *and* Teage: Hypſipyle, *his Wife, whom he he had deserted, hearing of his good success, and withall, of his Love-intrigue with* Medæa, *caused this Epistle to be sent to him.*

From So-hoe *Fields*, Feb. 27. 16$\frac{79}{80}$.

Husband,

THe Neighbours in our Alley do relate,
That at St. *Albans* you have won the Plate.
How easie a matter had it been for you.
T'have sent poor *Hyp.* your Wife, a *George* or two?
Did I, when *Flannel* was both dear and scarce,
Make you Trunk-hose to your ungrateful Arse;
I sew'd so long, my Fingers still do ake,
And, in all Conscience, I deserve my Snack.
I can hear something, though I keep at home;
I hear, y'have beaten *Teague* and *Whipping-Tom.*
You ran so swift, and strong, the People say,
You bore down all that stood but in your way:

Befor

Before your foundred Fellows could come up
You won the Match, and seis'd the *Caudle-Cup.*
I know, y' have been a Rogue, and done me (wrong;
Yet I'd hear this from your own flattring Tongue.
But why shouldst thou e'er hope for that, poor (*Hypsi*,
Since *Jason* loves a Bacon-visag'd Gipsey.
As I was washing, th'other day at door,
There came a Scoundril, ill-look'd Son-of-a-whore,
Who, jeering, ask'd if I were Madam *Jason*?
I'd like t'have thrown Soap suds his ugly Face-on.
Said I, I'm *Jason*'s Wife, for want of better;
Have you brought Money, from him, or a Letter?
How does he do? is he not very fine?
Come, come, let's see, I'm sure h'ath sent me Coin.
Quoth he, By God of Heaven, not a Souze;
He only bid me see you at your House.
The Fellow told m' a Tale of Cock and Bull;
At last, I ask'd about your Tawny-Trull.

H He

He ſaid, *Medæa*'s your beloved Gipſey.
And that your often ſeen together tipſey;
But, he believ'd 'twas but a Trick of youth:
A Trick; ſaid I, the Devil ſtop your Mouth.
Wound I had been laſh'd and whipt the City (round
That day I marry' thee, looſe Vagabond:
The Hangman in diſguiſe read Common-pray'r
When we were match'd, a very Hopefull Pair:
Curſt be the time I did admit you firſt,
And ſtrove to quench your everlaſting thirſt:
What Plague poſſeſt me when I brought you home?
This was no place to run with *Whipping-Tom*,
If I had taken but my Siſters counſel,
Y'had never ſet your flat-foot o'er the groundſel:
She bid me exerciſe the Fork and Spit;
We'd then good Goods, but now the De'il a bit,
'Twas well enough a year, nay, almoſt two;
What Fury hath poſſeſſion of you now?

Villain,

Villain, remember when you went away,
How often you Damn'd your self, you would not (stay;
And smoothly said, No place shall us divide;
A Curse upon your base dissembling Hide:
I was so big that I could hardly tumble,
Yet I believ'd your Oaths, and durst not grumble:
Said you, dear *Hypsi.* know that I am dead,
If I don't come before you're brought to bed;
You look'd like Air, with Breeches close to thighs,
I fancy'd you d be back within a trice:
When you were gone I to the Garret crept,
To see how nimbly o'er the Fields you tript;
As swift you went, so swift return you'ld make,
But all this haste was for that Bitche's sake:
Why do I rub my windows, wash my Room,
Expecting still your Rogueship would come home?
'Twould never vex me, if you were not seen
With such a damn'd confounded nasty Quean:

A Witch, a Bitch, in whom the Devil dwells,
Whose Face is made of Grease and Wall-nut-shells.
Master, quoth she, e'er from this Town you stir
You'll lose, (that is Your Pocket's pick'd by her.)
A plaguy Jade, who curses Night and Noon,
And houls, and heaves her Arse against the Moon,
Contemning her as Authress of the Flowers;
Railing at all our Sex, and Poxing yours:
No Childing Women doth in Travel linger,
But tow'rds her Pain the Fiend holds up a Finger:
She'll ride a Stick; when Sow is brought to bed,
Then Pigs have no more life than pigs of Lead:
She, with the Mother, at a door will wheedle,
And, in her Infant's heart, will stick a Needle:
This I believe, what e'er of me you think,
S' hath put some Rotten-post into your drink.
'Tis strange, that I should suffer all these wrongs
From her whom I would scorn to touch with (Tongs.

You'll

You'll lose the Name of beating *Tom* and *Teague*,
Whilst with this Whore you do continue League:
Nay, some do very confidently say't,
'Twas by her Witch-craft that you won the Plate:
Some think her Devil, others, new-laid Eggs,
Made you so fast advance your Bandy-leggs:
What can you find in such a Punck as she
Who from a Dunhill brings her Pedigree?
My Father dwells at Sign of *Golden-Can*,
An honest Vict'ler, a substantial Man:
'Tis true, they say, he is a drunken Sot;
What then; i'th' Parish he paies Scot and Lot:
Old *Bacchus*, the Wine-cooper, was my Grandsire;
Let her produce such Kindred if she can Sir:
Her Children have been gotten in a Bog.
By some large-pintled Wolf, or Mastive Dog:
My Babes were neither got nor whelp'd i'th' (Streets,
I labour'd for them 'twixt a pair of Sheets:

That they are yours, I'm ſure, you need not (doubt,
For they're as like as if y had ſpit them out:
Could they have gone, alone I'd made 'em amble
To your Apartment underneath a Bramble;
But I conſider'd how your Whore would treat ('em,
Nay, it is ten to one, the Hag would eat 'em;
Or elſe, perhaps, ſhe'd ſtick their tender Skins
All full of Sparables, or croocked Pins;
Since of her own s' hath murther'd many a Brat,
Would ſhe ſpare mine; oh! never tell me that.
Methink I ſee you and the hell-born Toad
Engendring in a Tree that's near the Road:
Suppoſe you were purſu'd, as y' are a Thief;
Where would you fly? where would you find (relief?
What if your ſelf and yonder Devil's dam
Should come to me, and try if you could ſham?

Sure

Sure I ſhould make you very welcome both,
And entertain you nobly by my Troth.
I ſhould towards you make ſome relenting (Heart,
But 'tis my Goodneſs more than your deſert:
And, for your Fire-brand there, that loathſome (Hag,
I would contrive the greateſt Pain and Plague:
Her Noſe being ſlit, to make her look more grim,
Like a *Spred-Eagle* on her Face ſhould ſeem:
Her coarſe black Skin ſhould from her Fleſh be (rent;
I'd run a Spit into her Fundament:
And, *Jaſon*, this thy Puniſhment ſhould be,
Thou ſhouldſt eat thoſe, ſo oft have ſwallow'd (thee.
But ſince it muſt not be I am contented
To let my Spleen in curſing her be vented:
May ſhe all Suſtenance for ever lack,
Untill ſhe takes her Child from off her Back,
And puts it in her belly for a Nuncheon,
And for the Fact be thrown into a Dungeon:

May ſhe be burnt to Cinders as a Witch,
And you be hang'd for loving of a Bitch.

Yours, as you have us'd her,

HYPSIPYLE.

For John Jaſon, *to be left at his Apartment, in a hollow Tree, between* Barnet *and St.* Albans.

PARIS

PARIS to HELLEN.

The ARGUMENT.

Paris *had liv'd a great while in Obscurity, at last being own'd by Alderman* Priam *a Rich Old Citizen, and receiv'd as his Son---he set up for a Gentleman; but very well knowing he could not be rightly accomplish'd without a Mistress, and hearing Fame speak* viva voce *in the praise of one* Hellen, *who liv'd somewhere in the* North. *He was at her house receiv'd, and during the absence of* Menelaus *her Husband, he endeavour'd to break his Mind to her; but being not thorough-pac'd in Gentility, his Modesty got the the upper hand of his Inclination, therefore he presently had recourse to his Pen, and writes her this conceited Letter.*

FReely and from my heart without compel- (ling,
I wish all health and happiness to *Hellen*:
For if yur're Sick, I'm sure to suffer pain;
As I'm a Lover and a Gentleman,

I need

I need not tell you that I'm off oth' hooks,
Your Ladiship discerns it by my Looks:
For you whose Eyes have such a piercing quick-(ness,
May see I'm overgrown in the Green-sickness;
So that upon the whole and perfect Matter,
I am your servant but I seem your Daughter.
I cou'd eat walls as well as white bred crum,
But fear to eat you out of house and home.
For this distemper I've read many Cures,
But the sole power of healing must be Yours.
Your Holiness (I cannot call you less,
That doth on Earth perform such Miracles,)
Your holiness I say within few weeks,
May fetch a lively colour in my Cheeks.
But if we are to long e're we begin,
I'm apt to fear it may corrupt within.
'Tis Love, 'tis Love, that makes me toss & tumble,
And in my Entrails does like Jollup rumble:

'Tis

'Tis as impossible you should not see't,
As 'tis to hide the Pox both small and great.
'Tis Love, You know th' effects of that disease,
Therefore pray fall to work when e're you please.
If at these Lines you do not jeer nor Jybe,
There is some hopes you may receive the Scribe.
And Madam know, I did engage the Stars,
Before I durst engage in *Cupid*'s Wars.
This is a grand affair, I had been silly
T'ave ventur'd on't whithout consulting *Lilly*:
To him I went for my own happy ends,
And all the Planets he hath made my Friends,
But above all, the most pellucid *Venus*,
Hath promis'd there should be a Job between us:
She knoweth best what's good for you and me,
She does command our Fates and Powers d'ye see.
Without her leave no living Lover stirs,
Paris, said she, put on your Boots and Spurs.

She

She did conſent I ſhould aſcend my horſe,
And toward your Manſion bend my glorious
(courſe.
Never by her was riding yet forbidden,
Her Goddeſs-ſhip with pleaſure has been ridden.
My heart's upon the racking trot---alas!
But ſhe can bring it to a Gentle pace.
Next, Madam, know, your Sight was no ſuprize,
I lov'd you by my Ears as well as Eyes.
Your Fame hath much out-ſounded the Report,
Of the great Guns at taking of a Fort.
I came not here to ſeek terreſtial pelf,
I made this progreſs for your heavenly ſelf.
The Womb o'th' Univerſe if I ſhould rifle,
To your more ſecret parts 'twere but a trifle.
To ſee your ancient Pile, I do not range,
We have more lofty Fabricks near th' Exchange.
'Twas for your ſake I ſpurr'd my ſtubborn Steed,
For you alone thro' thick and thin I rid.

You're

You're mine, what desperate mortal dares gain- (say't?
Sure I may take my Planet's word for that.
I fain would tell your Ladiship a Dream,
If it would not too great a trouble seem.
My Mother dream't, when she with me was quick,
She should bring forth a lighted Fagot---stick:
I am that Fagot-stick, I burn apace,
Oh quench me, Madam, in your watring---place.
I've taken fire at you, as a match at tinder;
Cool me, or else your Servant is a Cinder.
This was my Mother's dream, I now design,
Under Correction, to relate your mine.
I laid me down to sleep one Summers day,
Under the shade of a new Stack of Hay;
For we poor Lovers, such is our hard case,
Are glad to take a Nap in any place;
Three naked Ladies came, I well remember,
As naked as the Trees are---in *December*;

They

They told me they'd be judg'd alone by me,
Which was the moſt deſerving of the Three;
The firſt would bribe me with a Purſe of Gold;
My Judgment's neither to be bought nor ſold:
The ſecond offer'd me a Tilting Sword,
Knowing I ne're would take an angry word:
But ſayes the third, and in my face ſhe giggled,
With ſuch poor toyes you're not to be inveigled,
But if you value me above the reſt,
Then know young---man, you are for ever bleſt.
Within a little time you ſhall arrive,
Where a reſplendent Country Dame does live;
Firſt you muſt court her like an humble Beggar,
At laſt ſhee'll yield, and you may lay your Leg---(o're;
The Prize is yours, ſaid I, you ought to take't,
I kiſs'd her lower Parts, and ſo I wak'd.
My Dream is out, for thus I do explain it,
You are the Countrey Dame, and ſhe the Planet.

Without

Without delay I put on my accoutring,
And with full ſpeed, I came to you---a.---ſuitring.
But juſt as I was putting Foot in Stirrup,
Drinking with Friends a parting cup of Syrrup,
My Siſter came to th' door, a mad young Laſs,
Her name's *Caſſandra*, but we call her *Caſs*;
Brother, quoth ſhe, beware, beware, I ſay,
You do not meet a Fireſhip by the way:
A ſtrange wild Wench, I hope ſhe did not mean
That any where your Ladiſhip's unclean;
Heavens forbid, Good Soul, ſhe meant no more
Then flames of Love, as I have ſaid before.
Being arriv'd at this your decent houſe,
Whom ſhould I meet but your Illuſtrious Spouſe?
He brought a Tankard out of good March Beer,
Cold Pork and Butter, and ſuch houſhold chear;
He ask'd---if ever I Tobacco took,
I ſaid I'd take a pipe---but cou'd not ſmoak;

He

He ſhew'd m' his Garden, and his fine young (Trees,
His Barn, his Stable, and his houſe of Eaſe:
I ſaid 'twas wondrous pretty——but my mind
Still ran on what my Planet had deſign'd.
At laſt you came with ſuch a dazling grace,
I thought the Sun and Moon was in your face,
Lilly's and Roſes, Pinks and Violets,
Your looks were loaded with the vernal ſweets;
Your poor adorer was in ſuch amaze,
I vow and ſwear I knew not where I was;
Before I ſpoke I fell to private pray'r,
" Planet I thank the for thy tender care;
" Now thou haſt rais'd my Bliſs to ſuch a pitch,
" I humbly beg, that thou'dſt go thorough ſtitch.
At laſt I ſpake and bow'd in ſeemly wiſe,
And paid obeyſance to your ſparkling Eyes;
Your Beauty's greater than your fame did boaſt,
So is a May-Pole taller than a Poſt.

I've

I've heard, you once conferr'd your gracious fa-
(vour
On *Thefeus*, who was thought a cunning fhaver;
With him your Ladifhip has play'd fome Gambols,
Froliques y'have had, and many pleafant rambles.
But, by your Leave, your Lover was a Clown,
For leaving your bright Eminence fo foon;
D'ye think that *Paris* would have ferv'd you fo,
Would he have let Illuftrious *Hellen* go?
By *Stix* and *Acheron* your Servant fwears,
Rather than part with you, he'll lofe his Ears;
When that hour comes for which we both were
(born
And foon 'twill come, or Planet is forfworn;
When we fhall lye entranc'd——entranc'd I fay,
Then if you have the heart to go, you may;
Haften, forfooth, haften the happy Job,
For till't be done--— my heart will fhout and
(throb:

I 'Tis

'Tis very fit that you and I ſhould join,
Your Family's very good and ſo is mine.
My Father fin'd for Alderman, long ſince,
He's now grown rich, and lives like any Prince.
If you wou'd once make *London* your aboad.
You'd hate a Village as you'd hate a Toad.
Oh how your Ladiſhip wou'd ſtare to ſee
Our City Dames in all their Bravery.
They've Petticoats with Lace above their knees
Of Gold and Silver, or of Point *Veni-ce*;
Cornets and lofty Tow'rs upon the head,
And wondrous ſhapes of which you never read.
How ill a Pinner with a narrow Lace,
Becomes the Beauty of ſo bright a Face?
A fairer Face no mortal e're laid Lips to,
And I believe there are not whiter Hips too.
Too white to mingle with a Husband's thighes,
When I but think of that, my fleſh does riſe.

When

When towards me ſometimes a Glance does paſs,
Your poor Adorer looketh like an Aſs.
For if I ſhould return you Look for Look,
I fear your Husband will begin to ſmoak;
And I'll be hang'd, if ever *Menelaus*,
By any am'rous Look of mine, betray us;
Were it not at your Table I'd abuſe him,
For thruſting his great Paw into your Boſom:
That Watry Fiſt between your Breaſt does ſeem
Like a brown *George* dropt in a Bowl of Cream.
I'm mad to ſee him draw his Chair ſo cloſe,
And kiſs, and hugg you underneath my Noſe.
Then I go out, pretending to make Water,
Seeming to take no notice of the matter:
To all true Hearts I drink a Cup of Wine,
A Health that does imply both yours and mine;

Then ſeeming drunk,I tell ſome ſtrange Romance,
And lay the Scene in *Italy* or *France* ;
Of ſome bright Lady, and her brisk---Gall----ant;
By which two Lovers, you and I are meant.
But, Madam, to write more of this were non-
(ſence,
My Planet has contriv'd the bus'neſs long-ſince ;
By curious ſearch I ſomething can diſcover,
'Tis in your Blood---you're born to be a Lover.
What think you Lady, of your Father *Jove*?
Shew me a Town-bull h'as been more in Love.
Your Mother, *Læda*, too, who gave you ſuck,
H'as ſhe not been as good as ever ſtruk ?
When s'had a luſty Youth between her thighs,
What d'ee think ? would *Læda* cry to riſe ?
Your Parents being as right as ever piſt,
If you ſhould be preciſe, you wou'd be hiſt.

But

But if you muſt be conſtant to one Man,
With me to *London* make what haſt you can.
There wee'll provide a little Winter Houſe,
And you ſhall paſs for my renowned Spouſe.
By what I ſee your Husband does approve,
That in your Abſence here I ſhould make Love.
Or wou'd he elſe have gone,——under pretence,
To buy a Horſe---a hundred miles from hence?
The Bus'neſs ſeems to me, as plain a caſe,
As is the Noiſe upon your beauteous face.
To let you know that I ſhould be no clog,
Did he not ſay, Love me and love my Dog?
Nelly, ſaid he, be kind unto my Gueſt,
And let his entertainment be the *Beſt*.
I preſently his meaning underſtood,
If yours be not the *Beſt*—then nothing's good.
You ſee your Husband orders our affairs,
Therefore, dear Madam, do not hang an Arſe,

But let's away to *London*----*Crop* does wait,
Saddled and bridled at the Garden---gate;
Crop's a good Natur'd Beast---and carries double,
And will not think your Ladiship a trouble.
Strike while the Iron's hot, my Love is fervant,
Get up, and ride behind——

Your humble Servant

Paris.

HELLEN's

HELLEN's Answer to *PARIS*

The ARGUMENT.

Hellen *having receiv'd his Letter, at first seems wonderfully displeas'd at his Impudence, in attempting a Lady of her unspotted fame; who was bred and born in the Town where she liv'd, and was never call'd Whore. At length the Storm's over, and she Tacks about, giving him an assurance of her readiness to comply, but doubts her Gallent wo'not be constant. In plain English She's as willing as He.*

YOur Letter's wrot in such a filthy stile,
I did not think an answer worth my while,
Till I considere'd you might offer vi'lence,
And take advantage of a Woman's silence.
I'm sure you have not wanted drink or food,
I wonder in my heart you'll be so rude.

'Tis fine y'faith---becauſe you come from *London*,
You think a Country Body muſt be run down.
You of your Entertainment here may brag,
You were not us'd as if you'd had the Plague.
My Husband did receive you as a *Friend*,
And wou'd you to his Wife now prove a *Fiend*?
Perhaps you'll ſay of me, when you are gone,
Hellen! a Lady!——*Hellen*'s but a clown.
I'll one the name, ſince you can ſay no more,
I'd rather be a Clown, then call'd a Whore:
Yet for all that, though I keep Cows and Daries,
I can behave my ſelf as well as *Paris*.
Tho' I don't fleer like a young wanton Girle,
Yet you ſhall ſeldom ſee me frown or ſnarle.
Tho' you ſuch breeding, and ſuch manners own,
Let me deal plainly w'ye----I think you've none.
Or could you elſe believe me ſo untrue,
To leave my Spouſe and run away with you?

Becauſe

Becauſe a Fellow once did pick me up,
You think I'm to be ſtoln by every Fop.
He knew not whether I was Man or Woman,
But you conclude from thence that I am common.
When he perceiv'd *that I was none of thoſe*,
He very fairly brought me to my houſe.
And ſince I'm gotten quit of Maſter *Theſeus*,
Our *Paris* wou'd be nibbling too, God bleſs us !—
Though by my Trooth I cannot blame your Love,
If I were ſure that you wou'd conſtant prove,
Dy'e think I ſhould not be in dainty pickle,
If I ſhould run away with one that's fickle?
You urg'd to me th' example of my Mother,
As if the Daughter ſhou'd be ſuch another.
You don't conſider *Læda*, was betray'd,
By one that courted her in Maſquerade.
She thought ſh'ad met a harmleſs plum of feather,
But at *long-run* he prov'd a Stallion rather.

His

His Famili's the beſt in all the County,
All that you live by's but a Tradſman's bounty.
But that's all one, whereever love prevails,
Money's no more than pairing of my Nails.
Sometimes I think you love me when you look
With Eyes unmov'd, juſt like a Pig that's ſtuck.
And dabble with your fingers in my Palm,
And uſe to call the moiſture of it, —Balm.
If in the Glaſs I leave a little drop,
You'd ſay I'll drink your ſnuffs—and ſuck it up.
Hellen you carv'd with Penkife on the Gate,
And I wrot *Paris juſt a top* of that.
Theſe are ſhrewd ſigns of Love, and without (doubt,
You'd give a Leg or Arm to have a Bout.
Tho' you are not the firſt Man by a hundred,
That has ſeen me, and lov'd and gaz'd and won- (dred.
If you at firſt had come into our Town,
And courted *Hellen* in a Grogram Gown,

When

When I was but a ſilly Soul, God knows,
You might have made a Bridge of *Menel's* Noſe.
Now he commands in chief your Suit is vain,
To all true Lovers Marriage is a Bane.
But why ſhould *Paris* for a Miſtreſs long,
Since in your Sleep your Fancy is ſo ſtrong?
You can ſee three ſtark naked at a time,
And take your choice of Beauty's in a dream:
Yet you left Honour, Wealth, and God knows (what
And all for me—a pretty fancy that.
I know 'tis wheedle,—but if all were true,
It is no more than I would do for you.
You gueſs my want of Skill, by being ſo plain,
For I'am not us'd to write to any Man,
Except t' a Millener, (my Husband's Cozen)
Who ſends me Gloves,— and Ribbands by the (dozen.
Well—ſince it muſt be ſo—let's be diſcreet,
Let not our Town take notice that we meet;

For

For they ſuſpect already you're a Wencher,
There is not ſuch a place on Earth for Cenſure
Yet I can't ſee, why we ſhould be ſo nice,
I like you---by my Husband's own advice.
I cou'd not chuſe but laugh to hear him ſay,
Pray Love your Gueſt when I am gone away:
And all the while that *Menelaus* tarries.
You are committed to the charge of *Paris*,
The charge! Let us examine well the word,
Whether he meant your charge at Bed and Board;
Why ſhould he not mean both as well as one?
He knows---how much I hate to lye alone.
In my weak Judgment, 'tis an eaſie Caſe,
You are in all things to ſupply his place.
But for the Maſterſhip you're like to tug
Before you have me at the cloſeſt hug.
,Twill ſeem to me, if you ſome force do uſe,
As if I had a Maidenhead to loſe.

Lord!

Lord! how I write; if I were to be damn'd,
I cou'd not ſay't ——I ſhould be ſo aſham'd.
If I conſent I'll hold you any Money,
You'll ſerve me as you did you'r dear *Oenone*.
She hop'd ſhe ſhould be wedded in the Church,
Inſtead of that you left her in the Lurch.
But if we now were toward *London* jogging,
'Tis ten to one ſome Puppy would be dogging,
Or elſe ſome Neighbour on the Read wou'd ſtay (us,
And ask me after Mr. *Menelaus*.
Or we ſhall hear the Country-people ſay,
Would you believe that ſhe ſhould run-away?
Marry not hanſome Wives by this Example,
Since pretty Miſtreſs *Hellen*'s on the Ramble
I'm ſtrangly afraid of ſeeing Mr. *Priam*,
How I ſhall tremble when he asks whom I---am,
Tho' for my Life I ſhall not hold from Laughter,
If *Hecuba*, ſhould ſay Your Servant, Daughter

But

But above All 'tis *Hector* that I dread,
That *Hector* certainly will break my Head.
Who'd think you two from the same Mother
(came,
He's like a Lyon, you are like a Lamb.
Let *Hector* proser with his senseless huffing,
'Tis *knowing nothing now* that makes a Ruffian.
While *Paris* shall be skill'd in Lovers Arts,
And dive into our Sexes secret Parts;
Now you begin to think 'tis ten to one,
Your Suit is granted, and the Bus'ness done.
But not so fast,——consult my Friend *Clymene*,
No doubt—you'l make the Bus'ness up between
(ye
I'm loath to say't my self, she knows my mind,
And she can tell you how I am enclin'd.
When she informs you what must be transacted,
With too much Joy, I fear, you'l run distracted.

FINIS.

Books Printed for Richard Wellington.

THe Histories and Novels of the late Ingenious Mrs. *Behn* collected in on Volume, *viz.* *Oronoko*: Or the Royal Slave. The fair Jilt: Or Prince *Tarquine*. *Agnes de Castro*: Or the Force of Generous Love. Loves Watch: Or the Art of Love. The Ladies Lookinglass. The Lucky Mistake, and Letters never before Printed, with the Life and Memoirs of Mestriss *Behn*. Written by on of the fair Sex, *Price* 4 *s.*

Sir *Sam. Moreland's Vade Mecum*: Or the Necessary Companion. Containing, 1. A Perpetual Almanack, readily shewing the Day of the Month, and Moveable Feasts and Terms, for any Year past, present, or to come, curiously graved in Copper; with many useful *Tables* proper thereto. 2. The years of each King's Reign from the Norman Conquest compar'd with the Years of Christ. 3. Directions for every Month in the Year, what is to be done in the Orchard, Kitchin, and Flower-Gardens. 4. The Reduction of Weights, Measures, and Coins; wherein is a Table of the Assize of Bread. 5. A Table wherein any Number of Farthings, Half-pence, Pence, or Shillings, are ready cast up; of great use to all Traders. 6. The Interest and Rebate of Money; the Forbearance, Discompt, and Purchase of Annuities. 7. The rates of Post-Letters, both In-land and Out-land. 8. An Account of the Penny-Post. 9. The

The Principal Roads in *England*, ſhewing the diſtance of one Town from another in meaſured and computed Miles, and the diſtance of each from *London*; alſo the Market-Towns, on each Road, with the Days of the Week the Markets are kept on; as likewiſe the Hundred and County each Town ſtands in. 10. The Names of the Counties, Cities, and Borough-Towns in *England* and *Wales*, with the Number of Knights, Citizens, and Burgeſſes choſen therein to ſerve in Parliament. 11. The uſual and authorized Rates of Fairs of Coach-men, Car-men, and Water-men. The Sixth Edition with Tables for caſting up Nobles, Marks, Guineas, and Broad Gold.

Cocker's Decimal Arithmitick, The Second Edition, Corrected and Enlarged, by *John Hawkins.*

A new Body of Geography: Or a Deſcription of the Earth, containing by way of Introduction, the General Doctrine of Geography. 2. Deſcription of all the known Countries of the Earth, Account of their Situation, Bounds and Extent. 3. The Principal Cities and moſt Conſiderable Towns in the World; particularly an exact Deſcription, *&c.* 4. Maps of every Country in *Europe*, and a General Map of *Aſia*, *Africa* and *Amarica*, fairly Engraven'd on Copper, according to the beſt and lateſt Extant: And alſo particular Draughts of the Chief Fortified Towns of *Europe*: with an Alphabetical Table of the Names of the Places.

THE RAMBLE:

AN

ANTI-HEROICK

POEM.

Together with

Some Terreſtrial Hymns and Carnal Ejaculations.

By Alexander Radcliffe, *of Greys Inn, Eſq*

——*Semel inſanivimus omnes.*

LONDON,

Printed for the Author, and are to be ſold by *Walter Davis* in Amen Corner. 1682.

TO THE

RIGHT HONOURABLE,

JAMES

Lord Annesly.

My Lord,

THE onely pretence I had for making this mean Offer to your Lordship is, That your Lordship was pleas'd to excuse some of these loose Lines when

 they

they were in ſingle Sheets: Tho I muſt confeſs I propos'd a great Advantage, knowing that they ſhall live above the reach of Cenſure under your Lordſhips Protection, not without ſome Ambition of being known to your Lordſhip by the Title of,

Your Lordſhips moſt Humble and moſt Obedient Servant,

Alex. Radcliffe.

THE AUTHOR TO THE READER.

Honeſt Reader,

I*F I thought you would not ſmile immoderately, I cou'd tell you, That by the Command of ſome Honourable Perſonages,* Mark ye ! *and at the Requeſt of my Noble Friends,* D' ye mind me ! *theſe Trifles made* *a Sally into the World, ſtept into the Light, appear'd in this undreſs, or as a Modern Author has it, was Impetuouſly Hurried into the Preſs, (by which he verified,* Feſtinans Canis cœcos peperit catulos.*)*

This you know is the true Cant of many Prefacers; as who ſhould ſay, Gentlemen, my Book begs your pardon for this Intruſion. But if ſuch kind of Stuff will not paſs as an Excuſe for Publication, I'll tell ye what will; by chance I overheard an offer of ſome fooliſh Guinneys, and when those Toys are propos'd, such is our Human Frailty, we consent to the printing of any thing.

I have not further to say in the behalf of this Affair, since many of these things were wrote several years ago, when Youth and too much Money represented Extravagance a Virtue.

This is the last of this nature I shall ever own; the next shall be some Remarks upon the Life and Death of a true pious Protestant Dissenter, with the

the Excellency and Neceſſity of Perjury and Equivocation in a devout Separatiſt ; and that you'll ſay is a ſerious buſineſs.

— Paulo majora canamus.

God b'ye lovingly.

The

The Bookſellers Preface to his Cuſtomers.

Obliging Gentlemen,

THE *Ingenious Author having, next to his pleaſure of writing theſe Poems, taken care to Dedicate them to a Perſon of Honour, and alſo provided an Epiſtle to the Reader, hath left me nothing to do, but for my profit to print and to ſell them. But there having been ſome part of* The Ramble *formerly printed, under the notion of a Natural Preſumptive to my Lord* Rocheſter, *for Juſtice to that Noble Lord, as alſo for defending of Liberty and Property to my Author, whoſe Right as well as my own is invaded; I reſolved to bring an* Ha-

beas

beas Corpus, *and remove* The Ramble *home again, which was so falsly, maliciously, imperfectly, and feloniously made publick.*

I am likewise to tell you, that the foresaid Poem called The Ramble, *is here enlarged above two thirds more than heretofore you have seen it. I hope it will please you, good honest Gentile Reader; if so, it will sell; and if it sells, it will please me too; and so our little share of the world will naturally run in a concord, without tormenting our selves with Fears and Jealousies, or setting up for monstrous Whigs, Tantivy Tories, Abhorring Addresses, or other inferiour no Protestant Plots and Tory Plots. For my part (Gentlemen) I am resolved* (nemine contradicente) *to live in a whole skin so long as I can, hoping no* Irishman *will make a dead blow upon me; and I do hereby promise upon the word of an honest Stationer, that I will not endeavour to alter the Government, as it is established by Law either in Church or State. In fine, I am satisfied this Book of Poems hath no couched Treason in it, nor Arbitrary Power, and therefore I presume to Print it, without staying for the Suffrage of an Act of Parliament. Such as it is take it amongst you, and so God bless you all.* Vale.

The

The Contents.

NEws from Hell Page 1

As concerning Man 9

Have a care what you do 10

A Hard Caſe 13

The Canary Miſtreſs 15

What are you mad? 17

Money's all 19

Songs Burleſqu'd or Varied.

As Amoret and Phillis ſate 21

Hail to the Myrtle Shades 22

The poor Whores Song 24

Now now the Fights done 27

Tell me deareſt 28

Mr. Drydens *Deſcription of Night* 31

Diſdain yet ſtill I will love thee 32

Now at laſt the Riddle is expounded 33

To the Tune of Per fas per nefas 34

An Epitaph upon the worthy and truly vigilant Sam. Micoe *Eſq;* 35

Upon Mr. Bennet *Procurer extraordinary* 37

To

The Contents.

To a late Scotch Tune 39
Upon a Bowl of Punch 40
Upon the Pyramid 45
Upon a ſuperannuated Couple lately married 49
On the Proteſtants Flail 51
The Narrative 52
The fourteenth Ode of the ſecond Book of Horace 56
The tenth Ode of the ſecond Book of Horace 59
Horace's *well wiſhes to a ſcurvy Poet gone to Sea,* Epode 10. in Mævium 61
A Call to the Guard by a Drum 63
Dr. Wilds *humble Thanks for His Majeſty's gracious Declaration for Liberty of Conſcience* 74
Theſe for his old Friend Dr. Wild, *Author of the Humble Thanks, &c.* 81
The Ramble 85
The Lawyers Demurrer argued 110
The Swords Farwell upon the Approach of a Michaelmaſs *Term* 116
Wrote in the Banquetting in Greys Inn Walks 121

POEMS.

POEMS.

News from Hell.

SO dark the Night was that old *Charon*
Could not carry Ghoſtly Fare-on;
But was forc'd to leave his Souls,
Stark ſtript of Bodies, 'mongſt the Shoals
Of Black Sea-Toads, and other Fry,
Which on the Stygian Shore do lie:
Th' amazed Spirits deſire receſs
To their old batter'd Carcaſes;
But as they turn about, they find
The Night more diſmal is behind.

Pluto began to fret and fume
Becauſe the Tilt Boat did not come.

To the Shore's ſide he ſtrait way trudges
With his three Soul-cenſuring Judges,
Standing on Acherontic Strand,
He thrice three times did waft his Wand:
From gloomy Lake did ſtrait ariſe
A meager Fiend, with broad blew Eyes;
Approaching *Pluto*, as he bow'd,
From's head there dropt Infernal Mud;
Quoth he, *A tenebris & luto*
I come——'Tis well, quoth ſurly *Pluto*.
" Go you to t'other ſide of *Styx*,
" And know why *Charon*'s ſo prolix:
" Surely on Earth there cannot be
" A Grant of Immortality.
Away the wrigling Fiend ſoon ſcuds
Through Liquids thick as Soap and Suds.

In the mean while old *Eacus*,
Craftier far than any of us;

For mortal Men to him are ſilly;
Beſides he held a League with *Lilly*;
And what is acted here does know
As well as t'other does below:
Thus ſpake, " Thou mighty King of *Orcus*,
" Who into any ſhape canſt work us;
" I to your Greatneſs ſhall declare
" My Sentiments of this Affair.
" *Charon* you know did uſe to come
" With ſome Elucid Spirit home;
" Some Poet bright, whoſe glowing Soul
" Like Torch did light him croſs the Pool:
" Old *Charon* then was blithe and merry,
" With Flame and Rhapſody in Ferry.
" Shou'd he groſs Souls alone take in,
" Laden with heavy rubbiſh Sin;
" Sin that is nothing but Allay;
" 'Tis ten to one he'd loſe his way.
" But now ſuch Wights with Souls ſo clear
" Muſt not have Damnation here;

" Nor can we hope they'l hither move,
" For know (Grim Sir) they're damn'd above;
" They're damn'd on Earth by th' preſent Age,
" Damn'd in Cabals, and damn'd o'th' Stage.
" *Laureat*, who was both learn'd and florid,
" Was damn'd long ſince for ſilence horrid:
" Nor had there been ſuch clutter made,
" But that this ſilence did invade:
" Invade! and ſo 't might well, that's clear:
" But what did it invade?——an Ear.
" And for ſome other things, 'tis true,
" We follow Fate that does purſue.

A Lord who was in Metre wont
To call a Privy Member C——
Whoſe Verſe, by Women termed lewd,
Is ſtill preſerv'd, not underſtood.
But that which made 'em curſe and ban,
Was for his Satyr againſt Man.

A third was damn'd, 'cauſe in his Plays
He thruſts old Jeſts in *Archoe*'s days:
Nor as they ſay can make a *Chorus*
Without a Tavern or a Whore-houſe;
Which he to puzzle vulgar thinking,
Does call by th' name of Love and Drinking.

A fourth for writing ſuperfine,
With words correct in every Line:
And one that does preſume to ſay,
A Plot's too groſs for any Play:
Comedy ſhould be clean and neat,
As Gentlemen do talk and eat.
So what he writes is but Tranſlation,
From Dog and Patridge converſation.

A fifth, who does in's laſt prefer
'Bove all, his own dear Character:
And fain wou'd ſeem upon the Stage
Too Manly for this flippant Age.

A ſixth, whoſe lofty Fancy towers
'Bove Fate, Eternity and Powers:
Rumbles i'th' Sky, and makes a buſtle;
So Gods meet Gods i'th dark and juſtle.

Seventh, becauſe he'd rather chuſe
To ſpoil his Verſe than tire his Muſe.
Nor will he let Heroicks chime;
Fancy (quoth he) is loſt by Rhime.
And he that's us'd to claſhing Swords
Should not delight in ſounds of words.
Mars with *Mercury* ſhould not mingle;
Great Warriours ſhou'd ſpeak big, not jingle.

Amongſt this Heptarchy of Wit,
The cenſuring Age have thought it fit
To damn a Woman, 'cauſe 'tis ſaid,
The Plays ſhe vends ſhe never made.
But that a *Greys Inn* Lawyer does 'em,
Who unto her was Friend in Boſom.

So.

So not preſenting Scarf and Hood,
New Plays and Songs are full as good.

These are the better ſort I grant,
Damn'd onely by the Ignorant:
But ſtill there are a ſcribling Fry
Ought to be damn'd eternally;
An unlearn'd Tribe, o'th' lower rate,
Who will be Poets ſpite of Fate;
Whoſe Character's not worth reciting,
They ſcarce can read, yet will be writing;
As t'other day a ſilly Oafe
Inſtead of *Jove* did call on *Joſe*:
Whoſe humble Muſe deſcends to Cellars,
Or at the beſt to *Herc'les Pillars*.
Now *Charon* I preſume does ſtop,
Expecting one of theſe wou'd drop;
For any ſuch Poetick Damn'd-boy
Will light him home as well as Flambeau.

Eacus just had made an end,
When did arrive the dripping Fiend,
Who did confirm the Judges speech,
That *Charon* did a Light beseech.
They fell to Consultation grave,
To find some strange enlightned Knave.
Faux had like t'have been the Spark,
But that his Lanthorn was too dark.
At last th'agreed a sullen Quaker
Should be this business Undertaker;
The fittest Soul for this exploit,
Because he had the newest Light:
Him soon from sable Den they drag,
Who of his Sufferings doth brag;
And unto Heel of Fiend being ty'd,
To *Charons* Vessel was convey'd.
Charon came home, all things were well;
This is the onely News from Hell.

As concerning Man.

TO what intent or purpoſe was Man made,
Who is by Birth to miſery betray'd?
Man in his tedeous courſe of life runs through
More Plagues than all the Land of *Egypt* knew.
Doctors, Divines, grave Diſputations, Puns,
Ill looking Citizens and ſcurvy Duns;
Inſipid Squires, fat Biſhops, Deans and Chapters,
Enthuſiaſts, Prophecies, new Rants and Raptures;
Pox, Gout, Catarrhs, old Sores, Cramps, Rheums and Aches;
Half witted Lords, double chinn'd Bawds with Patches;
Illiterate Courtiers, Chancery Suits for Life,
A teazing Whore, and a more tedeous Wife;
Raw Inns of Court men, empty Fops, Buffoons,
Bullies robuſt, round Aldermen, and Clowns;

Gown-men which argue, and diſcuſs, and prate,
And vent dull Notions of a future State;
Sure of another World, yet do not know
Whether they ſhall be ſav'd, or damn'd, or how.

'Twere better then that Man had never been,
Than thus to be perplex'd: *God ſave the Queen.*

Have a care what you do.

I.

WHile Men endeavoured to adorn
The guilded Creſt of bloudy *Mars*,
Poor Love met with contempt and ſcorn,
Nor had he one Rag to his Arſe.

II.

His Wings were clogg'd with melting Snow,
Hardly ſupported by his Legs:

He

He had no ſtring left to his Bow,
His Arrows too had loſt their Pegs.

III.

I who had always ſeen him gay,
Wondered to find him thus diſtreſt;
I told him if with me he'd ſtay,
He might be welcom to my Breaſt.

IV.

With a faint Smile he ſhew'd his joy,
And ſoftly to his Lodgings crept,
Where ſome deſign diſturb'd the Boy,
He prattled all the time he ſlept.

V.

With a large Sigh his Soul I fill'd,
Which made a rumbling in his Guts;
Into his mouth I Tears diſtill'd,
Tears bigger far than Hazzle Nuts.

His

VI.

His ſtrength return'd to every Limb,
I let him round about me play;
I thought my ſelf ſecure of him,
Not dreaming he wou'd run away.

VII.

But this baſe perfidious Elf
Ungratefully from me did part,
Not onely ſtole away himſelf,
But took along with him my Heart.

VIII.

To *Cælia* then I did repair
With peremptory Hue and Cry,
Being aſſur'd this ſtolen Ware
Muſt light into her cuſtody.

IX.

IX.

She own'd it with obſequious art,
And drew on me this dire miſhap,
'Stead of returning me my Heart
She gave me a confounded Clap.

A Hard Caſe.

WHen trembling Pris'ners ſtand at Bar
In ſtrange ſuſpence about the Verdict:
And when pronounc'd they Guilty are,
How they're aſtoniſh'd when they've heard it!

When in a Storm a Ship is toſs'd,
All ask, What does the Captain ſay?
How they bemoan themſelves as loſt,
When his Advice is onely, *Pray!*

And

And as it was my pleaſing chance
To meet fair *Cœlia* in a Grove;
Both Time and Place conſpir'd t'advance
The innocent deſigns of Love.

I thought my happineſs compleat,
'Twas in her power to make it ſo;
I ask'd her if ſhe'd do the feat,
But (ſilly Soul!) ſhe anſwer'd, No.

Poor Pris'ners may have mercy ſhewn,
And ſhipwreck'd men may have the luck
To ſee their Tempeſts overblown,
But *Cœlia* I ſhall never

The

The Canary Mistress.

FOndling forbear, 'tis Heresie to think
There is a Mistress equal to thy Drink;
Or if in love with any, 't must be rather
With that plump Girl that does call *Bacchus* Father.
Thou mayst out-look, arm'd with her warm embrace,
Ten thousand Volleys shot from Womans Face,
Who wou'd withstand without this Aid Divine
Ten thousand times as many Tears of thine;
As many Sighs and Prayers would be her sport,
Exalted she so long maintains her Fort.
But when Diviner Sack hath fir'd thy Bloud,
Creating Flames which cannot be withstood;
To which is added Confidence as great
As his, that aim'd at *Joves* Celestial Seat;

Boldly

Boldly march on, not granting her the leisure
Of Parly; 'tis the Speed augments the Pleasure.
If she cry out, with Kisses stop her Breath;
She cannot wish to die a better Death.
Tell her the pleasant passages between
The God of War and Loves more gentle Queen.
When feeble *Vulcan* came, and in a fear
Lest they wou'd not continue longer there,
He chain'd 'em to the sport, with an intent
To keep such Lovers for a Precedent;
Glad to behold a tempting pleasure that
His weak Endeavours never could create.
Then stroke her Breasts those Mountains of De-
light,
Whose very Touch would fire an Anchorite.
Next let thy wanton Palm a little stray,
And dip thy Fingers in the Milky Way:
Thus having raiz'd her, gently let her fall,
Loves Trumpets sound, Now Mortal have at all.

A happy end thus made of all your ſport,
Lead her where every Lover ſhou'd reſort,
Where Madam *Sack*'s enthron'd, the tempting'ſt
That e'er was ſeated in a *Venice* Glaſs. (Laſs
Laſt, that this ſenſe of Pleaſure may remain,
Caſt away Thought and fall to Drink again.
Drink off the Glaſſes, ſwallow every Bowl,
And pity him that ſighs away his Soul
For that poor trifle Woman, who is mine
With one ſmall Gallon of Immortal Wine.
To get a Miſtreſs Drinking is the knack;
Love's grand exiſtence is Almighty Sack.

What are you mad?

I'LL mount my thoughts to Giant height,
I'm Conſtellation in conceit.
I'll pluck down *Sol*, and mount his Sphere;
Then ſullen *Daphne* ſhall appear,

And ſeeing me graſp *Phœbus* Rays,
Shall cringe and crown me with her Bays.
I'll rape the Moon, it ſhall be ſaid,
Cynthia hath chang'd the name of Maid;
Her twinkling Girles ſhall all be ta'en,
No Virgin left to bear her Train.
Thus conquering Sun, Moon, and Stars,
'Gainſt Gods themſelves I'll levy Wars.
Or if on Earth my Mind can reſt,
I'll be a Monarch at the leaſt.
Our dull Plebeians ſhall grow quicker,
Rincing their muddy Brains in Liquor.
The Miſer then ſhall ſcatter Caſh,
For Wine ſhall change his Balderdaſh;
And ſing and drink, and drink and ſing,
Till every Subject turns a King.
The conquer'd Gods ſhall make us Legs,
Intreating they may ſip the dregs.
Thus will we tipple till the World
Into Oblivion is hurld:

And

And when we feel old Age does come,
We'll poſt into *Elyſium* ;
And there our chiefeſt Joys ſhall be
To think of paſt Felicity.

Money's All.

BEauty is Nature's quaint Diſguiſe,
A Covert for the Game we hunt ;
Being pinch'd but once or twice it dies,
And leaves behind a ſlimy

Honour's the pleaſing Cheat of Men,
The White that does diſcover Blots ;
Like to the Plague at height, which then
Produceth gawdy purple ſpots.

Wiſdom the Souls grave penury,
Which he that owns dares not be brave ;

But with dull Morals muſt comply,
  Leſt the fond Age ſhould call him Knave.

But he whoſe Wealth ne'er knew a meaſure,
  May be truly termed free ;
For while he rules alone in Treaſure,
  He commands the other three.

Several

Several Late SONGS Burlesqu'd or Varied.

As Amoret and Phyllis sate, &c.

AS *Tom* and I well warm'd with Wine
Were sitting at the Rose,
In came Sir *John* with dire design
To ply us in the close.

The threatning Bumpers to remove
I whisper'd in his Ear;
Ah *Tom*, a bloody Night 'twill prove,
There is no staying here.
There is no, &c.

None ever yet had ſuch an art
In filling to the Brim;
Nor can you e'er expect to part,
If once engag'd with him.

Fly, fly betimes, for at this rate,
We certainly are ſunk:
In vain (ſaid *Tom*) in vain you prate,
I am already drunk.
I am already drunk.

Hail to the Myrtle Shades, &c.

PItty the private Cabal,
Ah pitty the Green Ribbon Club;
They've cut off poor *Strephon's* Entail,
And *Strephon* has met with a rub.

Strephon has ſtill the ſame Creatures,
Who fill him with many a doubt ;
But *Strephon* won't ſtoop to his Betters ;
Ah *Strephon*, ah why ſo ſtout!

Strephon once caper'd and pranc'd ;
Who but *Strephon* at Masks and at Balls!
Strephon the Saraband danc'd,
But *Strephon* now leads up the Brawls.
Strephon who ne'er had the skill
To uſe either Figure or Trope ;
For *Strephon* has no lofty Style,
Nor e'er was cut out for a Pope.

Strephon though not by his Tongue
Has drawn to him Parties and Factions,
People that make the day long
By buzzing of private Tranſactions.
Strephon has little to ſay,
But laughs at the Lord knows what ;

But the Club meets every day,
And ſits with eternal Chat.

The Poor Whore's Song, in alluſion to the Begging Souldier, Good your Worſhip caſt an Eye, &c.

GOod young Leacher caſt an Eye
Upon a poor Whores miſery:
Let not my antiquated Front
Make you leſs free than you were wont.
But like a noble Rogue
Do but diſembogue,
And you ſhall have our conſtant vogue;
For I am none of thoſe
That a bulking goes,
And often ſhows
Their Bridewell blows,

Or

Or New Prison Lash,
For filing of Cash,
Or nimming Prigsters of their Trash.

But I at Court have often been
Within the view of King and Queen;
A Guiney to me was no more
Than Fifteen Pence to a Suburb Whore:
And when he did tilt,
I did briskly jilt,
And swallow'd *Pego* to the Hilt.
A Pox was very near,
For *Bubo* did appear,
Had not my Surgeon then been there.

Once at the Bear in *Drury Lane*
The Bullies left me for a Pawn;
But I made my party good,
To Fifteen Guinneys and a Broad.

Oh you wou'd little ween
How that I have been
As great a Jilt as e'er was ſeen.
But if Mother *Bennet* came
With a Wheedle or a Flam,
She'd tell you how I cut the Sham.

From thence I march'd to *Creſwels* Houſe,
Under the name of a Merchants Spouſe;
And there I play'd the ſecret Lover,
Leſt jealous Husband ſhou'd diſcover.
Oh then came in the Rings,
And ſuch like things,
Which eldeſt Prentice often brings.
But now my poor ——
Contrary to its wont,
Muſt pocket any ſmall Affront.

Now

Now Now the Fight's done, &c.

NOw Now the Heart's broke,
Which ſo long has complain'd;
And *Clarinda* triumphs
In the Conqueſt ſh'as gain'd.
Love laughs at the ſight,
At the miſchief does crow;
For a Love-wounded Heart
Is to him a fine Show.
He plays up and down, and he ſports with the Heart,
And he ſhews it about on the point of his Dart.

But ſince the coy Nymph
So diſdainful is grown,

The power of her Charms
  We'll for ever disown;
We'll slight the fond Brat,
  Love no longer shall wrack us,
We'll shake off his Chains
  For the pleasures of *Bacchus*.
Then fill us more Wine, fill the Glass to the
    brim;
Thus we'll patch up our Hearts, they shall last
    our Life-time.

Tell me dearest pr'ythee do,
Why thou wilt and wilt not too, &c.

TEll me, *Jack*, I pr'ythee do,
  Why the Glass still sticks with you:
What does Bus'ness signifie,
If you let your Claret die?

Wine

Wine when firſt pour'd from the Bottle
  All its ſtrength and vigour flies;
So ſays ancient *Ariſtotle.*
    If it ſtand
    In your hand,
    It will then disband
  All its Spirits in a trice.
Who dares then refuſe to ſwallow
  All the Wine that out he puts,
Will find ſome heavy Judgments follow,
    Vinegar,
    Single Beer,
    Or ſuch diſmal Gear,
  To torment his wambling Guts.

Since to all ſubduing Wine
Lofty Arguments reſign;
He wrongs himſelf that ſits and prates
Of grave Matters or Debates.

Talk

Talk not then of Merchandizes,
Or what Intereſt may accrue
By Taxes, Subſidies, Exciſes,
Liberty,
Property,
Or Monopoly;
'Slife 'tis enough to make one ſpue.
Be as you were ever jolly,
Let it not ſtick at your door;
Bus'neſs is the greateſt folly.
Here's a Glaſs,
Let it paſs,
He's a formal Aſs,
That e'er talks of Bus'neſs more.

Mr.

Mr. Drydens *Description of Night.*

ALL things were huſh'd as Nature's ſelf lay dead,
The Mountains ſeem to nod their drowſie head;
The little Birds in Dreams their Songs repeat,
And ſleeping Flowers beneath the Night dew ſweat.
Even Luſt and Envy ſlept,&c.

Thus Burleſqu'd.

All things were huſh as when the Drawers tread
Softly to ſteal the Key from Maſters head.

The

The dying Snuffs do twinkle in their Urns,
As if the Socket, not the Candle, burns.
The little Foot-boy ſnoars upon the Stair,
And greaſie Cook-maid ſweats in Elbow Chair.
No Coach nor Link was heard, &c.

Diſdain, yet ſtill I will love thee; Nothing, &c.

FILL't up, yet ſtill I will take it;
Fill't up, I'll ne'er forſake it:
Although
My doom I know,
This Glaſs another will uſher,
Good faith it muſt be ſo,
Though drinking of this Bruſher,
I ſhall neither ſtand nor go.

Now

Now at last the Riddle is expounded, &c.

OLD *Beelzebub* was Father of Sedition;
Pride and Arrogance began division
In Religion,
And taught men to combine.
Fetch up the t'other double Bottle,
I will wash away design;
Bring a Spinster, though she have a hot Tail,
No Kingdom is enflam'd by Love or Wine.

The busie Party are the idle Fellows,
Fools that are suspicious and too jealous,
Let Hell loose,
The Devil's in 'em sure.
While he that drinks *de die & in diem*,
And all night hugs a Whore;

What Treaſon or Rebellion can come nigh
him,
Since he's employ'd each minute of an hour?

To the Tune of Per fas per nefas.

A Pox o' theſe Fellows contriving,
They've ſpoilt our pleaſant deſign;
We were once in a way of true living,
Improving Diſcourſe by good Wine.
But now Converſation grows tedeous,
O'er Coffee they ſtill confer Notes;
'Stead of Authors both learn'd and facetious,
They quote onely *Dugdale* and *Oats*.

A Traytor ſtill gives a denyal,
When a Glaſs is fill'd up to the beſt:
By drinking we know who is Loyal,
A Brimmer's the onely Teſt.

He

He that takes it 's untaunted of Treaſon,
He from all Impeachment is freed;
He may loſe his Feet for a ſeaſon,
But never ſhall loſe his Head.

An Epitaph upon the Worthy and truly Vigilant, Sam. Micoe *Eſq;*

HEre Honeſt *Micoe* lies, who never knew
Whether the Pariſh Clock went falſe or true.
A true bred *Engliſh* Gentleman, for he
Never demanded yet *Quel heur eſt il?*
He valued not the Riſe of Sun or Moon,
Nor e'er diſtinguiſh'd yet their Night from Noon.
Untill at laſt by chance he cloſ'd his Eyes,
And Death did catch him napping by ſurprize.

But firſt he thus ſpoke to the King of Fears,
Have I in Taverns ſpent my blooming years,
Outſate the Beadle nodding in his Chair,
Outwatch'd the Bulker and the Burglarer;
Outdrank all meaſure fill'd above the Seal,
When ſome weak Brethren to their Beds did reel;
And there when laſt nights Bottles were on board,
When Squires in Cloaks wrapt up in corners ſnoar'd;
I onely clad in my old Night Campain,
Call'd for more Wine and drank to 'em again?
Have I made Sir *John Robinſon* to yield,
Sent haughty *Langſton* ſtaggering from the Field?
And unto meager Death now muſt I ſink,
Death that eats all without a drop of Drink?
You ſteal my Life (grim Tyrant) 'cauſe you knew
Had I ſate up I'd kill'd more men than you.

Quoth

Quoth ſurly Death, *Statutum eſt, ſic dico*;
Sat vigilaſti——Bonos Nochios Micoe.

Upon Mr. Bennet, *Procurer Extraordinary.*

REader beneath this Marble Stone
Saint *Valentine*'s Adopted Son,
Bennet the Bawd now lies alone.

Here lies alone the Amorous Spark,
Who was us'd to lead them in the dark
Like Beaſts by Pairs into the Ark.

If Men of Honour wou'd begin,
He'd ne'er ſtick out at any Sin,
For he was ſtill for Sticking't in.

If Juſtice chiefeſt of the Bench
Had an occaſion for a Wench,
His reverend Flames 'twas he cou'd quench.

And for his Son and Heir apparent,
He cou'd perform as good an errand
Without a Tipſtaff or a Warrant.

Over the Clergy had ſuch a lock,
That he could make a Spiritual Frock
Fly off at ſight of Temporal Smock.

Like *Will 'ith' wiſp* ſtill up and down
He led the Wives of *London* Town,
To lodge with Squires of high renown.

While they (poor Fools) being unaware,
Did find themſelves in Manſion fair,
Near *Leic'ſter Fields* or *James's Square.*

Thus Wotthy *Bennet* was imploy'd ;
At laſt he held the Door ſo wide,
He caught a cold, ſo cough'd, and dy'd.

To a late Scotch Tune.

THomas did once make my Heart full glad,
When I ſet him up to rule at the Helm:
But *Thomas* has prov'd but a naughty Lad,
For *Thomas* I fear has betray'd my Realm.

I gave him a Houſe, I gave him Grounds,
I gave him a hundred thouſand pounds,
I gave him the Lord knows what Gadzounds:
But *Thomas*, &c.

The fineſt Courtier that e'er was ſeen,
He prais'd my Port, and he prais'd my Meen,

He prais'd all the Ladies at Court but the Q----
Yet *Thomas*, &c.

I gave him all Christian Liberty,
I let him sometimes lig by me,
I let him feel my Duchesses Knee,
Yet *Thomas*, &c.

Upon a Bowl of Punch.

THE Gods and the Goddesses lately did feast,
Where *Ambrosia* with exquisite Sawces was drest.
The Edibles did with their Qualities suit,
But what they shou'd drink did occasion dispute.
'Twas time that old *Nectar* shou'd grow out of fashion,
For that they have drank long before the Creation.

When

When the Sky-coloured Cloth was drawn from
the Board,
For the Chryſtalline Bowl Great *Jove* gave the
word.
This was a Bowl of moſt heavenly ſize,
In which Infant Gods they did uſe to baptize.

Quoth *Jove*, We're inform'd they drink Punch
upon Earth,
By which mortal Wights do outdo us in mirth.
Therefore our Godheads together let's lay,
And endeavour to make it much ſtronger than
they.
'Twas ſpoke like a God,——Fill the Bowl to
the top,
He's caſhier'd from the Skies that leaveth one
drop.

Apollo diſpatch'd away one of the Laſſes,
Who fetch'd him a Pitcher from Well of *Par-
naſſus.*

To

To Poets new born this Liquor is brought,
And this they ſuck in for their firſt Mornings
draught.

Juno for Limons ſent into her Cloſet,
Which when ſhe was ſick ſhe infus'd into
Poſſet;
For Goddeſſes may be as ſqueamiſh as Gipſies,
The Sun and the Moon we find have Eclipſes.
Theſe Limons were call'd the *Heſperian* Fruit,
When vigilant Dragon was ſet to look to't.
Six dozen of theſe were ſqueez'd into Water,
The reſt of the Ingredients in order come after.

Venus, th'Admirer of things that are ſweet,
And without her Infuſion there had been no
Treat,
Commanded two Sugar-loaves white as her
Doves,
Supported to th' Table by a Brace of young
Loves.

So

So wonderful curious these Deities were,
That this Sugar they strain'd through a Sieve
of thin Air.

Bacchus gave notice by dangling a Bunch,
That without his Assistance there could be no
Punch.
What was meant by his signs was very well
known,
So they threw in three Gallons of trusty Lan-
goon.

Mars a blunt God, who car'd not for dis-course,
Was seated at Table still twirling his Whiskers:
Quoth he, Fellow Gods and Celestial Gall-ants,
I'd not give a Fart for your Punch without
Nants;
Therefore Boy *Ganimede* I do command ye,
To fill up the Bowl with a Rundlet of Brandy.

Saturn of all the Gods was the oldest,
And you may imagine his Stomach was coldest,
Did out of his Pouchet three Nutmegs pro-
duce,
Which when they were grated were put to the
Juice.

Neptune this Ocean of Liquor did crown
With a hard Sea-Bisquet well bak'd by the Sun.

The Bowl being finish'd, a Health was began;
Quoth *Jove*, Let it be to our Creature call'd
Man;
'Tis to him alone these Pleasures we owe,
For Heaven was never true Heaven till now.

Upon

Upon the Pyramid.

To the Tune of Packington's Pound.

I.

MY Maſters and Friends, and good People
draw near,
For here's a new Sight which you muſt not
eſcape,
A ſtately young Fabrick that coſt very dear,
Renown'd for ſtreight body and *Barbary*
ſhape;
A Pyramid much high'r
Than a Steeple or Spire,
By which you may gueſs there has been a Fire.
Ah *London* th'adſt better have built new
Burdellos,
T'encourage She-Traders and luſty young
Fellows.

II.

II.

No ſooner the City had loſt their old Houſes,
But they ſet up this Monument wonderfull
tall;
Though when Chriſtians were burnt, as *Fox*
plainly ſhews us,
There was nothing ſet up but his Book in
the Hall.
And yet theſe men can't
In their Conſcience but grant,
That a Houſe is unworthy compar'd to a Saint.
Ah London, &c.

III.

The Children of Men in erecting old *Babel*,
To be ſaved from Water did onely deſire:
So the City preſumes that this young one is
able,
When occaſion ſhall ſerve to ſecure them from
Fire.

Blowing

Blowing up when all's done
Preſerves beſt the Town,
But this Hieroglyphick will ſoon be blown
down.
Ah London, &c.

IV.

Some ſay it reſembles a Glaſs fit for Mum,
And think themſelves witty by giving Nick-
names:
An Extinguiſher too 'tis fancied by ſome,
As ſet up on purpoſe to put out the Flames.
But whatever they ſhall
This Workmanſhip call,
Had it never been thought on 'thad been a
Save-all.
Ah London, &c.

V.

V.

Some Paſſengers ſeem to ſuſpect the grave
City,
As men not ſo wiſe as they ſhou'd be, or ſo;
And oftentimes ſay, 'Tis a great deal of pity
So much Coin ſhould be ſpent and ſo little
to ſhow.
But theſe men ne'er ſtop
To pay for going up,
For all that's worth ſeeing is when y'are atop,
Ah London, &c.

But O you proud Nation of Citizens all,
Suppoſing y'had rear'd but onely one ſtone,
And on it engrav'd a ſtupendious Tale,
Of a Conflagration the like was ne'er known:
It had been as good
T'have humour'd the Croud,
And then y'had prevented their laughing aloud.
Ah London, &c.

Upon

Upon a Superannuated Couple lately married.

I.

AN Aged Couple have combin'd,
And ſtock of years together joyn'd,
To vie with Time 'tis now deſign'd.

II.

Old Emblem with thy Sythe and Sand,
Thy canker'd power they do withſtand,
Nor Fate it ſelf ſhall here command.

III.

In vain will all their Projects be ;
Great Time, they muſt acknowledge thee,
When they endeavour *Rem in Re.*

IV.

They reprefent (each tedeous night,
When they their feeble force unite)
Methufalem th'Hermaphrodite.

V.

Of the grave Poffet made with Sack
A holy Sacrament they make,
Which they with like devotion take.

VI.

The dancing Guefts like Lightning flew,
This venerable Brace mov'd too
As Cripples in the Jovial Crew.

VII.

While Mufick play'd this folemn Pair
Kept time to every fprightly Air,
With deep-mouth'd Cough and hoarfe Catarth.

VIII.

VIII.

And now their wishes are complete,
With chaste desires in Bed they meet;
The Wedding seems a Winding sheet.

IX.

There let us leave them, there they're safe,
The next remove is to their Grave;
Epithalamium proves their Epitaph.

On the Protestants Flail.

IN former days th' Invention was of Wracks,
To dislocate mens Joynts and break their
Backs:
But this Protestant Flail of a severer sort is,
For *Lignum vitæ* here proves *Lignum mortis*.

The Narrative.

I.

COme prick up your Ears, if they are not
gone,
For this Deponent hath loſt his own ;
His Neck goes next 'tis forty to one,
Which no body can deny.

II.

Now this Deponent doth depoſe,
That he was once one of the Kings Foes,
But now he thanks God he's none of thoſe :
Sure our Deponent will lie.

III.

He ſwears that once there was *Harry* the
Eighth,

Who

Who was divorc'd from's firſt Wife *Kate*,
And that he cut off anothers Pate,
Which no body can deny.

IV.

Even ſo (quoth he) I can witneſs bring,
That the Q—— did conſent to the death of
the K——
But we are inform'd there was no ſuch thing;
For our Deponent will lie.

V.

He ſwears that before the Tower of *Babel*
Kain knock'd out the Brains of his Brother
Abel;
Here he ſwears to a Truth and not to a Fable;
Which no body can deny.

VI.

Even ſo (quoth he) ſome bloudy work

Was carried on by his Brother of *Y*——
But His Highneſs is neither a *Jew* nor a *Turk*,
For our Deponent will lie.

VII.

He ſwears that once in *Noah*'s time,
There was a great Floud that brought a great Stream,
And all were drown'd that cou'd not ſwim;
Which no body can deny.

VIII.

And now (God bleſs us) we're all in a fright,
For we had like t'have been ruin'd quite,
Our Throats ſhould all have been cut in the night;
But our Deponent will lie.

IX.

Further he ſwears that *S. Peter* from Heav'n,

Had

Had ſuch an abſolute power given,
That whom he pleas'd were condemn'd or for-
given,
Which no body can deny.

X.

Even ſo (ſaith he) Commiſſions went out
From the Pope to raiſe both Horſe and Foot,
That whom he pleas'd he might ſlaſh and cut;
But our Deponent will lie.

XI.

Some where or other S. *Paul* does aver,
That an Oath puts an end to all buſtle and ſtir,
By which he confirms it is lawful to ſwear;
Which no body can deny.

XII.

There was fooliſh ſwearing in former days,

But our Deponent has alter'd the case,
For 'has made more mischief than ever there was,
For our Deponent will lie.

The fourteenth Ode of the second Book of Horace.

Eheu fugaces, Posthume, Posthume,
Labuntur anni——

SEE, *Posthumus*, how years do fly;
Nor can the smoothest Piety
Fill up one wrinkle in the Face,
Or stop Old Ages certain pace,
Or quell Mortality.

When dying if thou shouldst design
To offer up at *Pluto*'s Shrine,

As

As many Bullocks ſat and fair,
As th'are days in every year,
One hour would not be thine.

See the thrice bulky *Geryon* ſtand,
Shackled in Ropes of *Stygian*:
On t'other ſide the doleful Pool
See the extended *Tityus* roul,
Where all Mankind muſt land.

This irkſom Shore muſt entertain
The greateſt Prince that e'er ſhall reign:
As great a welcom ſhall be there
Made to the meaneſt Cottager;
Diſtinctions are in vain.

In vain we ſhun the chance of War,
Where the moſt frequent dangers are.

In vain we do ſecure our ſelves
From troubled Seas, or Sands, or Shelves,
Or a cold Winter fear.

By all the Human Race at laſt
Muddy *Cocytus* muſt be paſt;
Where th'impious Daughters fill a Sieve,
Where Siſyphus in vain does ſtrive
To ſtick the Rowler faſt.

We bid Farwell to Land and Houſe,
To th' joys of an untainted Spouſe;
And to the ſilent Groves and Trees,
Whoſe Height and Shade at once do pleaſe:
But there ſad Cypreſs grows.

Then ſhall rich Wines brought from *Campain*,
Which you with Locks and Bolts detain,

Be

Be by your worthy Heir let looſe,
To give a Tincture round the Houſe,
Where he does entertain.

The tenth Ode of the ſecond Book of Horace.

Rectiùs vives, Licine, neque altum
Semper urgendo——

THat thou mayſt ſteer thy courſe with greater eaſe,
Plunge not far amidſt the deepeſt Seas:.
Or fill'd with horror when the Ocean roars,
Preſs not hard upon unequal Shores.
Who ever does admire the Golden Mean,
Is not pent up in Cottages unclean;
Inhabits not obſcure and ſordid Cells,
Nor courts the lofty Hall where Envy dwells.

The

The Pine Tree's vex'd by winds becauſe
'tis tall;
The higher the Tower, the greater is its fall.
By Heavens Artillery are Mountains ſhook,
And mightieſt Hills are ſooneſt Thunder
ſtrook.

In adverſe Times a well prepared Mind
With reaſon hopes a better change to find;
In proſp'rous days wiſhes no further good,
But modeſtly does fear Viciſſitude.

Heaven doth disfigure Earth with Winters
Rain,
And the ſame Heaven guilds the Earth again.
If at one inſtant things ſucceed not well,
There follows not an everlaſting Ill.
From Bow and Dart *Apollo* doth retire,
And ſometimes takes in hand his charming Lyre,
And by ſoft Notes excites the Female Quire.

When in ſome dangerous Straits your Barque
ſhall ride,

Let

Let never failing Courage be your Guide:
But if your Fortune blow auſpicious Gales,
Let Wiſdom then contract your ſtrutting Sails.

Horace's *well wiſhes to a ſcurvy Poet gone to Sea*, Epode 10. in Mævium.

Mala ſoluta navis exit alite,
Ferens olentem Mævium, &c.

WIth an unhappy Freight that Ship is ſtor'd,
That took the fulſom *Mævius* aboard.
Auſter remember what you have to do,
'Tis in your power to ſplit the Ship in two.
Eurus the Black, this your Command ſhall be,
To ſpoil the Tackle, and diſturb the Sea.

Aquilo

Aquilo riſe, and be your Fury ſhown,
As much as when you Trees have overthrown.
And in dark night no friendly Star appear,
As when *Orion* leaves the Hemiſphere.
Nor more of Calm at Sea let him enjoy,
Than conquering *Grecians* when they ſail'd
from *Troy*;
When *Pallas* to avenge the ſin of Fire,
By water made *Ajax*'s Crew expire.
What ſport 'twoud be t'obſerve the Sailers ſweat,
And ſee thy Earthen Face look paler yet!
To hear thy Howlings and unmanly Cries,
In vain beſeeching angry Deities!
Or let the Southern Winds drive thee away
Into the bellowing Gulph of *Adria*.
But if thy Carcaſe ſhould be caſt on ſhore,
That Cormorants the Carrion may devour:
To th' Tempeſts then a Holyday we'll keep,
By offering up a Ram or ſome black Sheep.

A Call

A Call to the Guard by a Drum.

RAt too, rat too, rat too, rat tat too, tat
rat too,
With your Noſes all ſcabb'd and your Eyes
black and blew,
All ye hungry poor Sinners that Foot Souldiers
are,
Though with very ſmall Coyn, yet with very
much Care,
From your Quarters and Garrets make haſte to
repair,
To the Guard, to the Guard.

From your ſorry Straw Beds and bonny white
Fleas,
From your Dreams of Small Drink and your
very ſmall eaſe,
From your plenty of ſtink, and no plenty of
room,
From your Walls daub'd with Phlegm ſticking
on 'em like Gum,
And Ceiling hung with Cobwebs to ſtanch a
cut Thumb,
To the Guard, &c.

From

From your crack'd Earthen Pispots where no
Piss can stay,
From Roofs bewrit with Snuffs in Letters the
wrong way ;
From one old broken Stool with one unbroken
Leg,
One Box with ne'er a Lid to keep ne'er a Rag,
And Windows that of Storms more than your
selves can brag,
To the Guard, &c.

With trusty Pike and Gun, and the other rusty
Tool ;
With Heads extremely hot, and with Hearts
wondrous cool ;
With Stomachs meaning none (but Cooks and
Sutlers) hurt ;
With two old totter'd Shooes that disgrace the
Town Dirt ;
With forty shreds of Breeches, and no one shred
of Shirt,
To the Guard, &c.

See they come, see they come, see they come, see
they come,
With Allarms in their Pates to the call of a Drum ;
Some lodging with Bawds (whom the modest
call Bitches)
With their Bones dry'd to Kexes, and Legs shrunk
to Switches ;

With

With the Plague in the Purſe, and the Pox in the
Breeches,
To the Guard, &c.

Some from ſnoring and farting, and ſpewing on
Benches,
Some from damn'd fulſom Ale, and more damn'd
fulſom Wenches;
Some from Put, and Size Ace, and Old Sim, this
way ſtalk;
Each mans Reeling's his gate, and his Hickup his
talk,
With two new Cheeks of Red from ten old
Rows of Chalk,
To the Guard, &c.

Here come others from ſcuffling, and damning
mine Hoſt,
With their Tongues at laſt tam'd, but with Faces
that boaſt
Of ſome Scars by the Jordan, or Warlike Quart
Pot,
For their building of Sconces and Volleys of Shot,
Which they charg'd to the mouth, but diſcharg'd
ne'er a Groat,
To the Guard, &c.

They for Valour in black too, the Chaplain does
come!
From his preaching o'er Pots now to pray o'er a
Drum.

All ye whoring and ſwearing old Red Coats
draw near,
Like to Saints in Red Letters liſten and give ear,
And be godly awhile ho, and then as you were,
To the Guard, &c.

After ſome canting terms, To your Arms, and the
like,
Such as Poyſing your Muſquet, or Porting your
Pike;
To the right, To the left, or elſe Face about;
After ratling your Sticks, and your ſhaking a
Clout,
Haſt your Infantry Troops that mount the Guard
on foot,
To the Guard, &c.

Captain *Hector* firſt marches, but not he of *Troy*,
But a Trifle made up of a Man and a Boy;
See the Man ſcant of Arms in a Scarf does
abound,
Which preſages ſome ſwaggering, but no bloud
nor wound;
Like a Rainbow that ſhews the World ſhan't be
drown'd;
To the Guard, &c.

As the Tinker wears Rags whileſt the Dog bears
the Budget,
So the Man ſtalks with Staff whileſt the Footboy
does trudge it

With

With the Tool he ſhould work with (that's Half
Pike you'll ſay;)
But what Captain's ſo ſtrong his own Arms to
convey,
When he marches o'er loaden with ten other
mens Pay?
To the Guard, &c.

In his March (if you mark) he's attended at leaſt
With Stinks ſixteen deep, and about five abreaſt,
Made of Ale and Mundungus, Snuff, Rags, and
brown Cruſt for,
While he wants twenty Taylors to make up the
cluſter,
Which declares that his Journey's not now to the
Muſter,
But to the Guard, &c.

Some with Muſquet and Belly uncharg'd march
away,
With Pipes black as their Mouths, and ſhort as
their Pay;
Whileſt their Coats made of holes ſhew like
Bone-lace about 'em,
And their Bandeliers hang like to Bobbins with-
out 'em,
And whileſt Horſemen do cloath 'em, theſe Foot-
ſcrubs do clout 'em,
For the Guard, &c.

Some with Hat ty'd on one ſide, and Wit ty'd on
neither;
Wear gray Coats and gray Cattle, ſee their Wenches run hither,
For to peep through Red Lettice and dark Cellar doors,
To behold 'em wear Pikes ruſty juſt like their
Whores,
As ſlender as their Meals and as long as their
Scores,
To the Guard, &c.

Some with Tweedle, wheedle, wheede; whileſt
we beat Dub a Dub;
Keep the baſe *Scotiſh* noiſe, and as baſe *Scotiſh*
ſcrub:
Then with Body contracted, a Rag open ſpread,
Comes a thing with red Colours, and Noſe full
as red;
Like an Enſign to the King, and to the Kings
Head,
Towards the Guard, &c.

Two Commanders come laſt, the Lieutenant perhaps,
Full of Low Country Stories and Low Country
Claps.
To be next him the other takes care not to fail,
Powder Monkey by name that vents ſtink by
whole ſale,

For

For where ſhould the Fart be but juſt with the
Tail
Of the Guard; &c.

And now hey for the King Boys, and hey for the
Court,
Which is guarded by theſe as the Tower is by
Dirt;
Theſe *Whitehall* muſt admit and ſuch other un-
houſe ye,
Each day lets in the drunk, whilſt it lets out the
drowſie,
And no place in the world ſhifts ſo oft to be lowſie.

Thank the Guard, &c.

Some to *Scotland-Yard* ſneak, and the Sutlers wife
kiſſes;
But deſpairing of Drink till ſome Countryman
piſſes,
And pays too (for no place in the Court muſt be
given)
To the Can-office then, all a *Foot-Soldier's* Heav'n,
Where he finds a foul *Fox*, ſoon, and cures Sir----

On the Guard, &c.

Some at Sh---houſe publick (where a Rag always
goes)

At

At once empty their Guts and diminish their
Clothes.
Though their Mouths are poor Pimps (Whore
and Bacon being all
Their chief Food) yet their Bums we true Cour-
tiers may call,
For what they eat in the Suburbs, they sh——
at *Whitehall*,
For the Guard, &c.

Such a like Pack of Cards to the *Park* making
entry,
Here and there deal an Ace, which the *Jews* call
a Centry,
Which in bad Houses of Boards stand to tell
what a clock 'tis,
Where they keep up tame Redcoats as men keep
up tame Foxes,
Or Apothecaries lay up their Dogs Turds in
Boxes.
Oh the Guard, &c.

Some of these are planted (though it has been
their lucks
Oft to steal Country Geese) now to watch the
Kings Ducks;
While some others are set in the side that has
Wood in,
To stand Pimps to black Masques that are oft
thither footing,

Just

Juſt as Houſewives ſet Cuckolds to ſtir their
Black Pudding.
Oh the Guard, &c.

Whileſt another true *Trojan* to ſome paſſage runs,
As to keep in the Debtors, ſo to keep out the
Duns;
Or a Prentice, or his Miſtreſs, with Oaths to
confound,
Till he hyes him from the Park as from forbid-
den ground,
'Cauſe his Credit is whole, and his Wench may
be found,
And quits the Guard, &c.

Now it's night, and the Patrole in Alehouſe
drown'd,
For nought elſe but the Pot and their Brains
walk the round;
Whileſt like Hell the Commanders Guard-cham-
ber does ſhew,
There's ſuch damning themſelves and all elſe of
the Crew,
For though theſe cheat the Men, they give the
Devil his due,
On the Guard, &c.

Whileſt a Main after Main at old Hazard they
throw,
And their Quarrels grow high as their Money
grows low;

Strait they threaten hard (using bad Faces for
Frowns)
To revenge on the Flesh, the default of the
Bones,
But the Blood's in their Hose, and in Oaths all
their Wounds.

Like the Guard, &c.

In the Morning they fight, just as much as they
pray;
For some one to the King does the Tidings convey
For preventing of *Murder*; Oh 'tis a wise
way!
Though not one of 'em knows (as a thousand
dare say)
That belongs to a dead man, unless in his
pay

For the Guard, &c.

With their Skins they march home no more hurt
than their Drums,
But for scratching of Faces, or biting of
Thumbs;
And now hey for fat *Alewives*, and *Tradesmen*
grown lean;
For the Captain grown *Bankrupt*, recruits him
again,

With

With ſending out Tickets, and turning out
Men

From the Guard, &c.

Strait the poor Rogue's caſhier'd with a Cane,
and a Curſe,
Fall from wounding no Men, now to cut ev'ry
Purſe:
And what then? Man's a *Worm*; theſe we Glow-
worms may name:
For as they'r dark of Body, have Tails all of
flame.
So tho' thoſe liv'd in Oaths, yet they die with
a *Pſalm*.

Farewell Guard, &c.

Dr.

Dr. Wild's *Humble Thanks for His Majeſty's gracious Declaration for Liberty of Conſcience*, Mar. 15. 72.

NO not one word can I of this great deed
In *Merlin* or old Mother *Shipton* read!
Old *Tyburn* take thoſe *Tychobrahe* Imps,
As *Silger*, who would be accounted Pimps
To the Amorous Planets; they the Minute know
When *Jove* did Cuckold old *Amphytrio*,
Ken *Mars*, and made *Venus* wink, and glances
Their cloſe Conjunctions and Midnight Dances;
When coſtive *Saturn* goes to ſtool, and vile
Thief *Mercury* doth pick his Fob the while;
When Lady *Luna* leaks, and makes her Man
Throw't out of Window into th'Ocean.
More ſubtil than th'Exciſemen here below,
What's ſpent in every Sign in Heaven they know.
Cunning

Cunning Intelligencers, they will not miſs
To tell us next year the ſucceſs of this;
They correſpond with *Dutch* and *Engliſh* Star,
As one once did with *CHARLES* and *Oliver.*
The *Bankers* alſo might have (had they gone)
What Planet govern'd the Exchequer known.
Old *Lilly*, though he did not love to make
Any words on't, ſaw the *Engliſh* take
Five of the *Smyrna* Fleet, and if the Sign
Had been *Aquarius*, then they'd made them Nine.
When *Sagittarius* took his aim to ſhoot
At Biſhop *Coſin*, he ſpied him no doubt;
And with ſuch force the winged Arrow flew,
Inſtead of one Church Stag he killed two;
Glocester and *Durham* when he eſpy'd,
Let Lean and Fat go together he cry'd:
Well *Wille Lilly*, thou knew'ſt all this as well
As I, and yet wouldſt not their Lordſhips tell.
I know thy Plea too, and muſt it allow,
Prelats ſhould know as much of Heaven as thou.

But

But now, Friend *William*, ſince it's done and paſt,
Pray thee give us *Phanaticks* but one caſt,
What thou foreſawſt of *March* the Fifteenth laſt;
When ſwift and ſudden as the Angels fly,
Th' Declaration for Conſcience Liberty;
When things of Heaven burſt from the Royal Breſt,
More fragrant than the Spices of the Eaſt.
I know in next years Almanack thou'lt write,
Thou ſawſt the King and Council over night,
Before that morn, all ſit in Heaven as plain
To be diſcern'd, as if 'twere *Charles's Wain.*
Great *B*, great *L*, and two great *AA's* were chief,
Under great *Charles* to give poor *Fan's* relief.
Thou ſawſt Lord *Arlington* ordain the Man
To be the firſt Lay-Metropolytan.
Thou ſawſt him give Induction to a *Spittle*,
And conſtitute our Brother *Tom Dolittle.*
In the *Bears* Paw, and the *Bulls* right Eye,
Some detriment to Prieſts thou didſt eſpy;

And

And though by *Sol in Libra* thou didſt know
Which way the Scale of Policy would go;
Yet *Mercury in Aries* did decree,
That *Wooll* and *Lamb* ſhould ſtill Conformiſts be.
But hark you *Will*, Steer-poching is not fair;
Had you amongſt the Steers found this *March-hare*,
Bred of that luſty Puſs the Good Old Cauſe,
Religion reſcued from Informing Laws;
You ſhould have yelp'd aloud, Hanging's the end,
By Huntſmens rule, of Hounds that will not ſpend.
Be gone thou and thy canting Tribe, be gone;
Go tell thy deſtiny to followers none:
Kings Hearts and Councils are too deep for thee,
And for thy Stars and *Dæmons* ſcrutiny.
King *Charles* Return was much above thy skill
To fumble out, as 'twas againſt thy will.
From him who can the Hearts of Kings inſpire,
Not from the Planets, came that ſacred Fire
Of Sovereign Love, which broke into a flame;
From God and from his King alone it came.

To

To the King.

So great, ſo univerſal, and ſo free!
This was too much, great *Charles*, except for thee;
For any King to give a Subject hope:
To do thus like thee would undo the Pope.
Yea tho his Vaſſals ſhould their wealth combine,
To buy Indulgence half ſo large as thine;
No, if they ſhould not onely kiſs his Toe,
But *Clements podex*, he'd not let them go:
Whileſt thou to's ſhame, thy immortal glory,
Haſt freed *All Souls* from real Purgatory;
And given *All Saints* in Heaven new joys, to ſee
Their Friends in *England* keep a Jubilee.
Suſpect them not, Great Sir, nor think the worſt;
For ſudden Joys like Grief confound at firſt.
The ſplendor of your Favour was ſo bright,
That yet it dazles and o'erwhelms our ſight:
Drunk with her cups my Muſe did nothing mind,
And untill now her Feet ſhe could not find.

Gree-

Greedineſs makes prophanneſs i'th' firſt place;
Hungry men fill their bellies, then ſay Grace.
We wou'd have Bonfires, but that we do fear
The name of *Incend'ary* we may hear:
We wou'd have Muſick too, but 'twill not do,
For all the Fidlers are *Conformiſts* too:
Nor can we ring, the angry Churchman ſwears
By the Kings leave the Bells and Ropes are theirs;
And let 'em take 'em, for our Tongues ſhall ſing
Your Honour louder than their Clappers ring.
Nay, if they will not at this Grace repine,
We'll dreſs the Vineyard, they ſhall drink the (wine.
Their Church ſhall be the Mother, ours the Nurſe;
Peter ſhall preach, *Judas* ſhall bear the purſe.
No *Biſhops*, *Parſons*, *Vicars*, *Curates*, we
But onely *Miniſters* deſire to be.
We'll preach in Sackcloth, they ſhall read in Silk;
We'll feed the Flock, and let them take the Milk.
Let but the *Blackbirds* ſing in Buſhes cold,
And may the *Jackdaws* ſtill the Steeples hold.

We'll

We'll be the *Feet*, the *Back*, and *Hands*, and they
Shall be the *Belly*, and devour the prey.
The Tythe-pig ſhall be theirs, we'll turn the Spit;
We'll bear the *Croſs*, they onely *ſign* with it.
But if the Patriarchs ſhall envy ſhow
To ſee their younger Brother *Joſeph* go
In Coat of divers colours, and ſhall fall
To rend it 'cauſe it's not Canonical;
Then may they find him turn a Dreamer too,
And live themſelves to ſee his Dream come true.
May rather they and we together joyn
In all what each can; but they have the Coyn;
With *prayers and tears* ſuch Service much avail;
With *tears* to ſwell your *Seas*, with *prayers* your
Sails;
And with Men too from both our Parties; ſuch
I'm ſure we have can cheat or beat the *Dutch*.
A thouſand *Quakers*, Sir, our ſide can ſpare;
Nay two or three, for they great Breeders are.
The Church can match us too with Jovial Sirs,
Informers, *Singingmen*, and *Paraters*.
Let the King try, ſet theſe upon the Decks
Together, they will *Dutch* or *Devil* vex.
Their Breath will miſchief further than a Gun,
And if you loſe them you'll not be undone.
Pardon, Dread Sir, nay pardon this courſe Paper,
Your Licenſe 'twas made this poor Poet caper.

ITER BOREALE.

Theſe

These for his Old Friend Doctor Wild, *Author of the* Humble Thanks, &c.

SIR,

HAD I believ'd report, that ſaid
These Rhymes by Doctor *Wild* were made,
I long before this time had ſent
Some ſymptoms of our diſcontent.
For ſince y' have left off being witty,
Your *humble thanks* deſerves our pitty.
I can't imagine what you'l do,
Your Muſe turn'd *Non-conformiſt* too?
And will not eaſily diſpence
With the old way of writing ſence!
She hath receiv'd, if that be true,
As much *Indulgence* then as you.

Surely (*Dear Sir*) you did not pray
Since you convers'd with *Tycho Brah.*
Jove play'd the wag, and *Luna* pist,
Do these things with *Free-Grace* consist?
Celestial Signs serve to express
The good man's heav'nly mindedness;
There are but Twelve of them in Heaven,
Yet he'll name one by one eleven;
And if you're not in too much hast,
'Tis ten to one, he names the last.
You had been horribly put to't,
If *Sagittarius* could not shoot:
Aquarius and the *Smyrna* Fleet,
I'll swear, a very good conceit.
But, Doctor, let us know, why will ye
Thus vex your self at *William Lilly*?
Tis true, he could not find it out,
That *March* would bring all this about;

But

But on that day you well might gather
That there would be ſome change of weather:
And change of weather in a Nation
Portends a kind of alteration.

This favour, you do ſay, did come
Fragrant and full of all perfume,
Like Eaſtern Spices (it ſhould ſeem)
This had done rarely in a Theme.
To the next Column ----- let us ſee
How you diſcourſe His MAJESTY.
Where every ſolemn Epithite
Does look like Grace before you eat,
Which being ſaid, as rudely you
Do take the Boldneſs to fall to,
With Rhymes moſt reverently ſent
About *Pope Clement*'s Fundament,
And *Puns* that would provoke the hate
Of any under Graduate.

Peter Non-con (it ſeems) muſt pray,
And *Judas* Church muſt take the Pay.
Some angry men would call him rude Aſs,
That calls the Church of *England Judas*,
You'l be no *Biſhop*, nor no *Curate*,
'Tis only Miniſter that you 're at.
Miniſter ! It ſounds, methinks,
Like Paſtor *Clark* of *Bennet Fynks*.
These Favours which the King doth heap
Upon your Head, hath made you *leap*.
And ſince y' have found your feet again,
The *Gout's* got up into your *Brain* :
If *cap'ring* be ſo fine a thing,
Pr'ythee come over for the King.

Your humble Servant,

OBEDIAH.

Ill Painters when they make a Sign
Either of Talbot or of Swine,
To ſatisfie all Perſons rogant,
That they might make a Hog or Dog on't;
Do never think it any ſhame
To underwrite the Creature's Name.
WILD *made ſome Verſes you muſt know,*
ITER BOREALE *is below.*

THE
RAMBLE.

WHile Duns were knocking at my Door,
I lay in Bed with reeking Whore,
With Back ſo weak and P---- ſo ſore,
You'd wonder,

I rouz'd my Doe, and lac'd her Gown,
I pin'd her Whisk, and drop't a Crown.
She pist, and then I drove her down,
Like Thunder.

From Chamber then I went to dinner,
I drank ſmall Beer like mournful Sinner,
And ſtill I thought the Devil in her
Clitoris,

I ſate at *Muskats* in the dark,
I heard a Tradeſ-man and a Spark,
An Atturney and a Lawyer's Clark,
Tell Stories.

From thence I went, with muffled Face,
To the Duke's Houſe, and took a place,
In which I ſpu'd, may't pleaſe his Grace,
Or Highneſs ;

Shou'd

Shou'd I been hang'd I could not chuſe
But laugh at Whores that drop from Stews,
Seeing that Miſtris *Marg'ret* -------
So fine is.

When Play was done, *I* call'd a Link,
I heard ſome paltry pieces chink
Within my Pockets, how d'ee think
I' employ'd 'em?

Why, *Sir*, I went to Miſtriſs *Spering*,
Where ſome were curſing, others ſwearing,
Never a Barrel better Herring,
per fidem,

Seven's the main, 'tis Eight, God dam 'me,
'Twas ſix, ſaid I, as God ſhall ſa' me,
Now being true you cou'd not blame me
ſo ſaying,

Sa' me! quoth one, what Shamaroon
Is this, has begg'd an Afternoon
Of's Mother, to go up and down
A playing?

This was as bad to me as killing,
Miſtake not Sir, ſaid I, I'm willing,
And able both, to drop a ſhilling,
Or two Sir:

Goda'mercy then, ſaid Bully *Hec* ----
With Whiskers ſtern, and Cordubeck
Pinn'd up behind, his ſcabby Neck
To ſhew Sir.

With mangled fiſt he graſp'd the Box,
Giving the Table bloody knocks,
He throws ---- and calls for Plague and Pox
T' aſſiſt him;

Some

Some twenty ſhillings he did catch,
H'ad like t'have made a quick diſpatch,
Nor could, Time's Regiſter, my Watch
Have miſt him.

As Luck would have it, in came *Will*,
Perceiving things went very ill,
Quoth he, y' ad better go and ſwill
Canary,

We ſteer'd our courſe to *Dragon Green*,
Which is in *Fleetſtreet* to be ſeen,
Where we drank Wine---not foul---but clean
contrary.

Our Hoſt, y'cleped *Thomas Hammond*,
Preſented ſlice of Bacon Gammon,
Which made us ſwallow Sack as Salmon
Drink water,

Which

Being o'er-warm'd with last debauch,
I grew as drunk as any Roch,
When hot-bak'd-Wardens did approach,
Or later,

We broke the Glasses out of hand,
As many Oaths I'd at command
As *Hastings*, *Sabin*, *Sunderland*,
Or *Ogle*,

Then I cry'd up *Sir Henry Vane*,
And swore by God I would maintain
Episcopacy was too plain
A juggle.

But oh! the damn'd confounded Fate
Attends on drinking Wine so late,
I drew my Sword on honest *Kate*
O'th' Kitchin,

Which

Which *H*-----'s Wife would not endure,
I told her tho' ſhe look'd demure,
*S*he came but lately I was ſure
From Bitching.

A Club there was in t'other Room,
I bolted in, being known to ſome,
Such men are not in Chriſtendom
For jeſting,

They uſe a plain familiar ſtile,
Appearing friendly all the while,
Yet never part without a Broil
Inteſtin.

The firſt as Steward did appear,
A ſtrange conceited Barriſter,
Who on all Matters will infer
His Reading,

A Band 'had on, that's very plain,
A Velvet Coat, a ſhining Cane,
Some Law, leſs Wit, and not a grain
Of Breeding.

The Company were in a fit
Of talking News about *Maeſtricht*,
How that the Prince's leaving it
Was ſudden,

Quoth he, (becauſe they ſhould ſay
That he knew leſs of this than they)
Juſt ſuch a caſe I read this day
In *Plowden.*

An angry Captain that was there,
Could Indignation not forbear,
'Zounds, ſayes he, did Man e're hear
Such Non-ſence ?

We

We talk of Sieges, Camps, and Forts,
This Fool's a keeping Country Courts,
With musty Law and dull Reports,
Damn'd long since,

Go bolt your Cases at the Fire,
From *Plowden*, *Perkins*, *Rastal*, *Dyer*,
Such heavy stuff does rather tire
Than please us:

Tell not us of Issue Male,
Of Simple Fee, and Special Tail,
Of Feofments, Judgments, Bills of Sale,
And Leases.

Can you discourse of Hand-Granadoes,
Of Sally-Ports and Ambuscadoes,
Of Counterscarps and Pallizadoes,
And Trenches,

Of

Of Bastions, blowing up of Mines,
Or of Communication Lines,
Or can you guess the great Designs
The *French* has?

The Barrister began to start
To hear such bloody terms of Art,
And did desire with all his heart
A Farewel;

Till younger Member of the House,
Resenting this as an Abuse,
Thought it convenient to espouse
His Quarrel.

This was a spruce young Squire that
Knew the true Manage of the Hat,
And every morning ty'd Cravat
With Project:

One

One that was ſure he knew the Town,
To men of Fringe and Feather known,
'Mongſt whom all Law he wou'd diſown,
And Logick.

Captain, quoth he, I'll tell you thus:
You are miſtaken much in us,
With dint of Sword we can diſcuſs;
'Tis true Sir,

You trail'd a Pike, or ſome ſuch thing,
In *Holland*, here you huff and ding:
And all the Town (forſooth) muſt ring
Of you, Sir.

I can remember you at *Lambs*,
Whither you'd come with forty ſhams;
And ſwore you wou'd renounce all Games
But Tennis:

Laſt

Laſt night (ſuch luck ne'r man had yet)
You play'd with Counteſs at Picquet,
And that ſhe did (by Jeſus) get
Twelve Guinnies ;

Nay worſe --- juſt parting with my Lord,
He fancy'd much your Silver Sword,
And you wear his not worth a Turd ----
--- A Bawble ;

But for the Hilt he's like to pay,
For you will have his Iron Grey :
A ſwifter Nag is not this day
In ſtable.

And all the great deſign of this
Is but to borrow half a Piece,
Or be excus'd (if Ready miſs)
From Clubbing :

The

The Captain ſwell'd, yet did not know
Whether the Youth would fight or no,
Or if 'twere ſafe to give the Foe
A drubbing.

Company's here, and for their ſake,
Quoth he, ſome other time I'll take,
For I did never love to make
A Buſtle,

Even when you pleaſe, quoth Younker, then
I'm every Evening to be ſeen
'Mongſt witty Coffee-drinkers in
Street Ruſſel.

One that was Doctor, Rook, and Quack,
With whom the Captain us'd to ſnack,
Becauſe he'd make the firſt attack
On Bubble.

Did think it fit to do him right,
Altho' he knew he would not fight,
Yet Cully he would ſore affright
And trouble.

Therefore the Captain's part he took;
Home Lad, quoth he, unto your Book,
If Letters fail, Go Bully-rock
The Carrier,

For here you muſt not vent your ſtuff,
We underſtand you well enough:
You muſt not think to rant and huff
A Warrier.

I knew when *Animal* and *Ens*
Was once the chief of your pretence,
But now you think y'ave ſprucer Senſe
And Knowledge.

When

When first this Town y' arriv'd unto,
The only Bu'ness y' ad to do
Was to enquire out those that knew
Your Colledge.

Certainly Mortal never saw
A thing so pert, so dull, so raw,
And yet 'twou'd put a Case in Law,
If they wou'd,

Then it began to visit Playes,
And on the Women it wou'd gaze,
And looked like Love in a Maze,
Or a Wood.

Into Fop-corner you wou'd get,
And use a strange obstreperous Wit,
Not any quiet to the Pit
Allowing:

And when my Lord came in, you'd ſpy,
If toward you he caſt an Eye,
Y' had lucky opportunity
Of bowing,

At laſt you got a ſwinging Clap,
Which ran upon you like a Tap,
And lay for Cure of this miſhap
At *Tooting*,

Then you writ Letters of Advice
To Parent, for ſome freſh ſupplies,
Pretending to the exerciſe
Of Mooting:

At length you underſtood a Dye,
Carry'ing in Fob variety
Of Goads, of Bars, of Flats, of High
And Low-Dyce.

But

But when you hear the fatal doom,
That Father ſhall remand you home,
It hardly will appear you come
From Studies.

The Youth was juſt a throwing Glaſs
Of Wine into the Doctor's Face,
When Barriſter took Heart of Grace,
And courage:

Doctor, ſayes he, you are a Cheat,
A greater Knave walks not the Street,
A verrier Quack one ſhall not meet
In our Age.

Doctors of Phyſick we indeed
Do moſt abominably need:
If you are one, that ſcarce can read
A Ballat,

You ſerv'd a Doctor,—true, from whom
You ſtole Receipts, being his Groom,
Or waiting on him in his Room,
As Valet.

On Serving-men you us'd to cut,
Giving 'em the high Game at Put,
And made the Fellows ſtill run out
Their wages,

With Chamberlain you quit old ſcores,
Ruin the Tapſter at all-Fours,
And ſtill obſerve the Carriers-hours,
And Stages.

T' Apothecary next you go,
To whom your ſtollen Receipts you ſhow,
That y'ave no Learning he does know,
And ſmall Parts:

Yet

Yet for Advantage does proclaim
You as the eldeſt Son of Fame,
And ſwears your Cures have got a Name
In all Parts.

Then take your Lodgings at his Houſe,
With care and ſecrecy to chouſe
Thoſe Fools incurable, that thus
Are minded,

If y'are deſir'd to write a Bill,
Your Eyes have a defluxion ſtill,
That if you do but touch a Quill,
You're blinded.

'Mongſt gilded Books on ſhelves you ſqueeze
Old *Gallen* and *Hippocrates*,
For ſuch learn'd men (ſay you) as theſe
I'll ſtickle.

Tho' what they were you cannot tell,
Giants they might have been as well,
Or two Arch-Angels, *Gabriel*,
And *Mich'el.*

In ſhort, you are an empty Sawſe ---
Before this word quite out he draws,
The Doctor ſtruck him croſs the Jaws,
God bleſs us!

The Student then propos'd a flap,
Which on Quack's beſt of Eyes did hap,
With might and main-- on Youth fell Cap--
---tain *Beſſus.*

I'th' Room was Juſtice *Middleſex*,
Who underſtanding Statute *Lex*,
Being unwilling to perplex
A Riot,

Softly

Softly as he could ſpeak, did cry,
(Which no Body obſerv'd but I)
My Friends, in Name of Majeſty,
Be quiet.

The Youngſter firſt deſir'd a Truce,
Becauſe Cravat from Neck hung looſe,
Captain, quoth he, your Weapon chooſe,
I'll fight 'ee:

Nay then, thought I, if ſo it be,
You're very likely to agree,
There's no Diverſion more for me,
Good night t'ee.

And having now diſcharg'd the Houſe,
We did reſerve a gentle Souſe,
With which we drank another rouſe
At the Bar:

And

And good Chriſtians all attend,
To Drunkenneſs pray put an end,
I do adviſe you as a Friend,
And Neighbour.

For lo! that Mortal here behold,
Who cautious was in dayes of old,
Is now become raſh, ſturdy, bold,
And free Sir;

For having ſcap'd the Tavern ſo,
There never was a greater Foe,
Encounter'd yet by *Pompey*, No
Nor *Cæſar*.

A Conſtable both ſtern and dread,
Who is from Muſtard, Brooms and Thread,
Preferr'd to be the Brainleſs Head ---
O' th' People,

A

A Gown 'had on by Age made gray,
A Hat too, which as Folk do ſay,
Is ſirnam'd to this very day
A Steeple ;

His Staff, which knew as well as he,
The Bus'neſs of Authority,
Stood bolt upright at ſight of me ;
Very true 'tis,

Thoſe louzy Currs that hither come
To keep the King's Peace ſafe at home,
Yet cannot keep the Vermin from
Their *Cutis.*

Stand ! ſtand ! ſayes one, and come before ----
You lye, ſaid I, like a Son of a Whore,
I can't, nor will not ſtand, ---that's more---
D'ye mutter ?

You

You watchful Knaves, I'll tell what,
Yond' Officer i'th May-pole Hat,
I'll make as drunk as any Rat,
Or Otter.

The Conſtable began to ſwell,
Altho' he lik'd the motion well:
Quoth he, my Friend, this I muſt tell
Ye clearly,

The Peſtilence you can't forget,
Nor the Diſpute with *Dutch*, nor yet
The dreadful Fire, that made us get
Up early,

From which, quoth he, this I infer,
To have a Body's Conſcience clear,
Excelleth any coſtly cheer,
Or Banquets;

Beſides,

Besides, (and 'faith I think he wept)
Were it not better you had kept
Within your Chamber, and have slept
In Blanquets :

But I'll advise you by and by,
A Pox of all advise, said I,
Your Janizaries look as dry
As *Vulcan* :

Come, here's a shilling, fetch it in,
We come not now to talk of Sin,
Our Bus'ness must be to begin
A full Can.

At last, I made the Watch-men drunk,
Examin'd here and there a Punk,
And then away to Bed I slunk
To hide it,

God

God ſave the Queen, --- but as for you,
Who will theſe Dangers not eſchew,
I'd have you all go home and ſpue
As I did.

The Lawyers Demurrer *argued.*

By the Loyal ADDRESSERS (the Gentlemen) of Grays-Inne, *againſt an ORDER made by the Bench of the ſaid Society.*

To the Tune of *Packington's* Pound, Or, *The Round-head Reviv'd.*

I.

DEar Friends, and good People, with Gowns, and with none;
I'll tell you a Tale of a parcel of *Whiggs*,
The Spawn of ſome *Rebells* in year Forty One,
Who, like their damn'd Sires, purſue their Intrigues:
It

It occasions amazing,
That some Members of *Grays Inn*, (Raising:
Turn Tail to their King, from whom they'd their
You Mortals of Law be confounded for ever,
Who refuse an Address made to your Law-giver.

II.

By a musty old Custom, call'd Order of Pension.
Giving Thanks to the King was judg'd an Affray,
And straight they Decreed, 'twas just to Dis-bench One, (S)
For shewing himself more Loyal than they:
So thus the *Dom. Com.*
Speak loudly for some, (Mum.
But propose the King's Int'rest the word shall be
You Mortals of Law be confounded for ever;
Who refuse an Address made to your Law-giver.

III.

III.

Men of the Sword they ſay make a Diviſion, (S)
And militant Lawyers their Wiſdoms diſown,
So that from the King to have had a Commiſſion,
Does not conſiſt with a tatter'd old Gown:
These men make pretence,
Both to Law and to Senſe, (Prince,
Yet ſay the Law's broke, if you fight for your
You Mortals of Law be confounded for ever,
Who refuſe an Addreſs made to your Law-giver.

IV.

(out,
From th' Ancients (they urge) this Order comes
And therefore expect a ready Obedience,
But how can that be, ſince their Maſterſhips doat,
And they themſelves have forgotten Allegiance:
Therefore let's pray,
Both by Night and by Day,
That they may Conform, and then we'll Obey.

You

You Mortals of Law be confounded for ever,
Who refuse an Addrefs made to your Law-giver.

V.

But wou'd it not move a Heart made of Flint,
To think that a Houſe muſt continue no longer,
Since the grave Gubernators refus'd to conſent,
Except 'twere propos'd by a Bar-Iron-monger; (C)
Or elſe by a Brewer, (O)
Who ſerves them with Beer,
So ſmall, that they'r fill'd with Suſpicion and Fear.
You Mortals of Law be confounded for ever;
Who refuſe an Addreſs made to your Law-giver.

VI.

Now ſome of the younger diſconſolate fry, (G)
As if they'd been ſtill at --- *Quæſo Magiſter*,
Under ſuch ſtrange Apprehenſions did lye,
They deſir'd to conſult the Chappel-Miniſter,

I One

One of the young men,
Wou'd not handle a Pen,
For my Lord and my Father won't take me agen.
You Mortals of Law be confounded for ever,
Who refuse an Addreſs made to your Law-giver.

VII.

The number of thoſe who refus'd to ſubſcribe,
Are fitly compar'd to the days of poor *Job*,
Few and Evil --- and of a Satanical Tribe,
Who ſcandalize all the reſt of the Robe;
Thoſe of the Bar-meſs,
Who cry'd --- No Addreſs,
Found their Party of Faction were two to one leſs:
You Mortals of Law be confounded for ever,
Who refuſe an Addreſs made to your Law-giver.

VIII.

Now you have heard of theſe *Lawyers Demurrer*,
And how their weak Arguments are over-rul'd,
Without all Diſpute will think an *Abhorrer*,
Of them and Petitions, are loyally bold.
For ſuch Impudence,
Both at Bar and at Bench,
Proceeds from thoſe Men who their King would Retrench;
You Mortals of Law be confounded for ever,
Who refuſe an Addreſs made to your Law-giver.

The SWORD's *Farewell, upon the approach of a* Michaelmas-Term.

HEalth to my Friends, a terror to my Foes,
Revenging Wrongs, impatient of blows,
Couragious Metal, trueſt of all Steels,
Sure to thy Maſter, always at his heels;
Ready to jog him by the Elbow, when
He is confronted by the Sons of Men.
Soul of my Weapon, thou ſhalt take thy Reſt;
And acquieſce within thy Sable Neſt,
One Month muſt fix thee in a certain Station,
Thy Maſter's *Term* muſt prove thine own *Vacation*:
Till that's expir'd (his Honour be thy Pawn)
Though here thour't hang'd yet thou ſhalt not be (drawn,
Thou ſhalt not now too late at Night appear,
T'incenſe the King's Almighty Officer,
Nor vex his Watch, leſt by his great Command,
They knock thy Maſter down, and bid him ſtand:

Nor

Nor fly at Mortal wight, though ne're ſo tall,
Who paſſing by Surrenders not the Wall,
Nor puſh at Bayliffs ſtout denouncing War:
We know no Sergeants now but at the Bar.
They're fix'd (but with ſuch moveable devotion,)
Come when you will, you'l find them in a Motion.
Not willing any Man ſhould be oppreſt,
'Tis only *Judgment* that they would Arreſt.
Thou ſhalt not now be bare, when *Hector* cloaths,
And backs the Lye with rags of ſwelling Oaths,
Now ſuch great words admit a Period,
He muſt ſpeak only truth, *ſo help him God*;
The Stile is chang'd, (the Seaſon ſo will have it)
If he will ſwear, 't muſt be by *Affidavit.*
Thou muſt not now come forth in view, as once,
To fright a Rev'rend Bawd, and build a Sconce,
Nor make a Drawer ſtand all Night to Skink
Full cups, and watch to fill thy Maſter Drink,
To rubiſie his Cheeks, though when he will,
He can take out a *Fieri Facias* ſtill.
Or Preſidents (if common Writs do fail,)
Direct to me a ſpecial Writ of *Aile.*

(Whilom at ſuch a Sign conven'd the Wits ;
But now no Sign is known except for Writs)
Thou muſt forbear a while at *Inn* and *Inn*,
T' out-brave whom thou ſuſpecteſt like to win:
No jogging chance muſt now blind mortal Eyes,
We'll find freſh Bail of *Men* and not of *Dice*.
Pray for an Action now, and not an *Ace*,
Let every *Deuce* Produce a Debtor's caſe:
And in the ſtead of every *Trey* that's thrown,
So many *Tryals* may we call our own.
To caſt a *Quatre* now we muſt forget,
And call to mind a *Quare Impedit*.
Each *Cinque* a *Capias*, and for every *Size*
Wiſh that a *Scire Facias* may ariſe.
Now we muſt think *Hazard* brings little gain,
Throw a *Mandamus* rather than a *Main*;
On certainties 'tis ſafeſt to rely,
More's gain'd by *Bill*, than gotten by the *By*.
To *Play-Houſes* thou now ſhalt bid adieu,
Although the Farce be gay enough and new,
Ne're before Acted, brings thee not among
Thoſe that ſell Two and Six-pence for a Song.

No

No Idle Scenes. fit busie times as these,
Instead of *Playes* we now converse with *Pleas*;
And 't's thought the last do savour more of Wit,
For those have Plots to spend, but these to get.
(Give way, Great *Shakespear*, and immortal *Ben*,
To *Doe* and *Roe*, *John Den* and *Richard Fen.*)
Farewel (dear Sword) thour't prov'd, and laid aside;
Thy youngest Brother, *Penknife*, must be try'd;
That thou art best, needs but a thin dispute,
Thou woundest skin of *Man*, he skin of *Brute*,
'Tis pity such an Urchin long should Reign
To raze a Line, when thou can'st prick a Vein.
'Tis thou can'st make such horrid bloody work
Will fright the Pope, and scare the biggest *Turk*;
Thy very name will make a Cripple run
Swift as a Courtier from a City Dunn.
Now *Tom* (in Acres rich, is come to Town)
To change the Title of a Yeoman's Son,
Thou bid'st him kneel, and stroak'st his empty Skul,
And mak'st him rise *Sir Thomas* Worshipful:
Thus thou mak'st special Knights of common men,
When he hath made his best 'tis but a Pen;

Yet

Yet ſuch a Pen, that when't has learn't it's Trade,
It may undo the Knight which thou haſt made.
  That thou art monſtrous valiant is too certain,
For inſtance this, in fine (as ſaith Sir *Martin*)
Th'haſt kill'd---But ſoft, ſome wiſer are than ſome,
I ſhould *Marr-all* if I diſcover whom.
In point of Honour this, (deny't who can)
Thou never turn'dſt thy *Back* to any Man:
The ſhort and long on't's thus, I'll ſafely ſay,
Though thou ſhould'ſt *break*, thou would'ſt not (run away:
Yet 'twould not wound thy credit long, for when
The *Term* is done, I'll ſet thee up agen.

Cedant ARma togæ, concedat laurea linguæ.

Wrote

Wrote in the Banquetting-Houſe in Grayes-Inn-Walks.

HERE Damſel ſits diſconſolate,
Curſing the Rigor of her Fate,
Till Squire Inſipid having ſpy'd her,
Takes Heart of Grace, and ſquats beſide her.
He thus accoſts, ---- Madam, By Gad
You are at once both fair and ſad.
She innocently does ſubmit
To all the Tyrants of his Wit.
The Bargain's made, ſhe firſt is led
To the three Tuns, and ſo to Bed.

But yonder comes a graver Fop,
With heavy Shoe, and Boot-hoſe-top;
To him repairs a virtuous Sir,
Whoſe Queſtion is, What News does ſtir?
With Face askrew, he then declares
The probability of Wars:

And

And gives an ample ſatisfaction
Of *Engliſh*, *French*, and *Dutch* Tranſaction.
Thus chattering out three houres Tale,
They tread to th' Mag-pye, to drink Ale.

Death and the old man.

A Paraphraſe upon one of Æſop's Fables.

A Poor old man, who had by cleaving wood,
Full threeſcore years procur'd a livelihood;
He never ran the various riſques of Fate,
Each day his ſhoulders bore an equal weight,
Till now at laſt of Age he did complain,
And thought each Load did weigh as much again.
One Evening coming home he made a ſtop,
And wanting ſtrength, he let his Burden drop;
Then ſate upon it, with a proud neglect,
And ne're till now did on himſelf reflect.
What Being's this call'd Man, and what am I?
One of the Drudges of Mortality.

I've

I've cut down Wood enough, now Death attend,
And to my Life and Labour put an end:
With that the Grifly Skelleton appear'd,
And the old man was from his Senſes ſcar'd:
Quoth Death, Old fellow, if you'd ſpeak with me,
I'le give a period to your miſery:
Oh No, ſweet Sir, quoth the amazed Grandſire,
I wiſh it not, as I'me a living man Sir;
I only did deſire, becauſe I'me weak,
And cannot lift this Burthen to my Neck,
That you'l be pleas'd, to lend a helping hand,
And I am yours, *hereafter*, to command.

Moral.

Silly old Wretch, who living art oppreſt,
Yet dar'ſt not venture on Eternal reſt.

Upon the Death of Edward Story, Esq; *Master of the* Pond, *and Principal of* Bernards-Inn.

LET all that read these Lines in Tears be (drown'd,
Since *Story*'s dead, the Master of the *Pond*;
What idle Tales fantastick Poets feign
About God *Neptune*, and his stormy Main,
That his Dominion's great, 'tis no such matter,
What great Command can there be over Water?
To *Story*'s power 'twere Non-sence to compare it,
For he was Master of a *Pond* of *Claret*:
And he this Scarlet *Sea*, like *Moses*, --- did
To all his Club of *Israelites* divide:
And when too late at night some came in doz'd,
The *Pond* o'er them, as o'er th' *Egyptians* clos'd.
This *Pond* was *Helicon*, where *Story* sate
Like mighty *Phœbus*, in his Chair of State:
His Tongue made Musick like *Apollo*'s Lyre,
Which when he us'd, he silenc'd, all the Quire;
He had his Muses too, but more than Nine,
Besides, they're of the Gender Masculine:

Of

Of different Subjects every Muſe did ſing, (bring.
Which they from *Johns*, or *Grays-Inn* Walks did
Some Foreign Matters ſang, another Muſe,
In humble Stile, ſang of Domeſtick News;
Some ſang of bloody Plots againſt the Throne
And Government; another ſang of none;
Till by ſome ſign his pleaſure was expreſt,
Then all were quiet while he told a Jeſt.

And as this witty Club he kept in awe,
He headed too, a Body of the Law;
Yet for all that, as skilful as he was,
Death brought his *Action* without ſhewing *Cauſe*.
And ran him to the *Utlary* with ſuch ſpeed,
He had not time enough to ſuperſede.
With all Mankind *Death* muſt his *Intereſt* clear,
But to call in the *Principle*'s ſevere.

Upon the Memory of Mr. John Sprat, *late Steward of* Grayes-Inn.

CAN any man in reaſon think it fit
That Death ſhould eat a *Steward* at a Bit?
And in *one long Vacation* ſhould devour,
What, in all Conſcience, might have ſerv'd for *four*?
Had it been *Term-time* he'd have taken courſe
To have repell'd both him and all his Force.
Villainous Death! he would have plac'd a Chop
With every Dart that thou haſt in thy Shop:
Thou durſt not then attempt him (meager Glutton)
When he and's men were arm'd with *Beef* & *Mutton*;
Thou wert afraid to nibble at *John Sprat*
While *Barrel-Cod* and *Whitings* were in date,
His Voice disbanded thee, and all thy Troop,
When gracefully he gave the word, *Serve up*.
'Twas cowardly to take him, when *Raw Fruits*,
When *Turneps*, *Cucumbers*, and *Cabbedge Roots*
Had chill'd his Blood: he had defi'd being ſick,
Had he ſurviv'd the time they call *Tres Mich'*.

But

But why had not thy hungry Maw been eas'd,
If *Tosborough* or *Taylor* thou hadſt ſeiz'd;
Thoſe *ſingle parts* of *Middle-piece* and *Rump*,
Inſatiate thou! to fall upon the *Chump*.
Since *buſie Sprat* (our Lives Truſtee) is dead,
The *Bottled* Joyes of *Norfolk* too are fled:
The *Thetford-Ale*, which won the hearts of Youth,
And made them chant his praiſe with open mouth:
Whom afterwards he'd greet in friendly ſort,
Your Chamber, Sir, I think's in Coney Court.
When will't be opportune----to bring my Bill?
D'ſliſe, ne'r talk of that man; when you will.
Then he (good man) who alwayes knew his time,
To Chamber-door would in the Morning climb.

Now truſty *Sprat* is gone, there will not come
So Generous a Steward in his Room:
He would in *younger Brothers* ſtill confide:
Whoſe Parents do in Foreign Lands reſide:
He entertain'd them well; yet did not know
Whether their Friends were living there or no.
They ſcorn'd to come as *Commoners* to eat,
But took it as the *Noble Steward's Treat.*

Ah,

Ah cruel Hag! (though Muſe be out of breath,
Yet ſee! ſhe'l have one parting blow at Death)
Were there not equal Standers of the Hall,
That thou didſt call *Sprat* in a *private Call*?
And, which is worſe, by Tyrannous permiſſion,
He did go out before he did *petition*.
Some Preſidents 'tis likely we ſhall find
Upon the Roll of *Commons* left behind;
Which his *ſurviving* Friends (without a *Bribe*,
It is believ'd) are willing to tranſcribe:
Therefore 'tis hop'd (leſt *Youth* ſhould be perplext)
That his *Executors* may *Go out* next.

His Epitaph.

BEneath this Stone, Reader, there lieth flat
Upon his Back the truſty *Steward Sprat*:
Diſturb him not, for if he chance to ſtir,
He'll ſay, *When ſhall I wait upon you, Sir*?

FINIS.